The Separation Myth

The Relative World Belief – II

POWERFUL NEW TEACHINGS FROM "A COURSE IN MIRACLES"

Sharon Moriarty

Jesus Christ

GATEWAY TO ETERNITY PUBLICATIONS

http://www.GatewayToEternity.com

ISBN (Paperback) : 978-0-9971179-5-0

Library of Congress Control Number (LCCN) : 2016920862

GATEWAY TO ETERNITY PUBLICATIONS

http://www.GatewayToEternity.com

THE SEPARATION MYTH

DEDICATION

DEDICATED TO

SKYWALKER

FOR HIS INSPIRATION

THE MYTH OF SEPARATION

Perhaps, you think this is a story about love and heartbreak and to some extent it is. Only this love story took a very twisted and fateful turn a few million years back.

Back then, we had it made! We were sublime creators in the pure and potent realm of the Absolute. A realm so highly charged and throbbing with life that it can find no parallels to our earthly experience. Knowing ourselves only as perfect creations in a Kingdom of light, we were surrounded by unconditional love and happiness. As in the Utopian paradise of Shangri-La, we were immersed everlastingly in the sacred womb of celestial wonderment, ecstasy, and awe. The world of shadows, demons, psychic-vampires and other chimerical monstrosities was entirely unknown. For here, there were no bodies, time or meaningless things. No pain, suffering or loss. No source of interference to disrupt our unassailable peace.

Regrettably, those born with a silver spoon are often the most contemptuous. When everything comes spontaneously, there is frequently a powerful impulse to throw it all away. We blew it for we became ungrateful of all the gifts our divine Creator heartily bestowed and the power he so freely shared. We wanted to have things entirely our own way and be totally free of all dependence. So one day, the dark thought arose that perhaps we could expropriate all our Father's power and glory for our own idle purposes. Employ them to fashion private kingdoms in which we alone ruled. Alien empires of the mind obsessed with the pursuit of meaningless temptations, lusts, and petty reprisals. Ones in which our supreme authority, eminence, and specialness would be beyond all doubt. In effect, we wanted to usurp our Heavenly Father's throne and get rid of the old man for good—eject him entirely out of the equation of our lives.

This unloving thought was enough to introduce the very first stain of guilt into our luminous and immaculate minds. Immediately, afterward, we realized that love is only powerful, only so long as it is wholly shared. Once one tries to hoard, contain or limit it in any way, it soon loses all its meaning. Yes, Love only works through complete inclusion. Wherever there is even a hint of exclusion or rejection, it entirely disappears. Unadulterated Love is a dish we have not tasted consciously since. All we faithfully imbibe, in its name, is that obsessive, manipulative and selfish ego concoction that masquerades as Love.

Nonetheless, it was already too late. Our unholy thought became a fatal coup de grâce that we were powerless to undo. That one instant, in which Love became lost from our awareness, was enough to trigger a fearful, cheerless and meaningless world of separation, to come into apparent being. From that moment onward, we became deeply embedded in the relative world of spacetime and form. A dispiriting nowhere land spun out of the threadbare fabric of illusions. One where madness and mayhem know no end. An arbitrary psychotic luniverse with no intrinsic value or prevailing excellence. Alas! This is where we seem to find ourselves now. Even though it is an illusory kingdom of the mind, no one is laughing anymore. Instead, each takes themselves to be a tragic figure mercilessly trapped and bound, in a dream of their own making. Deeply conditioned by fear, hate, and desire, no one doubts now the overly complex and terrifying world of their perceptions. Unfortunately, since we take this world far too seriously, we cannot break free of its deadly toxic grip.

Love and Knowledge remain safe deep in our hearts and minds. These eternal gifts, the dark cloud of guilt is powerless to ever extinguish. However, denial has pushed our original guilt deeply underground, firmly out of our awareness. The continued power it forcibly executes on

our minds seems to guarantee that we will remain ensnared in its twisted web of deception. Very few are pre-
pared to expose their inner thoughts of guilt to the light of
true forgiveness. Nevertheless, the Eternal Kingdom continues to shine in all its original brilliance and splendor. Its
presence only goes undetected because of our failures to
forgive. Once we decide to cleanse and purify our minds,
the memory of our unalterable perfection will be restored
to our awareness.

The real can never be lost. Our immortality is beyond all
question, and our Father never abandoned us. His eternal
Kingdom still remains our Divine Inheritance. What appears lost in time is not irredeemably lost. Our chronic
states of confusion, delusion and disillusionment can only
temporarily cover our immortality over. We can choose,
whenever we wish, to undo the dreary and comfortless
world of our perceptions because we are the ones who
fabricated it. The most expeditious way to dispel all illusions is by deciding to no longer invest in them.

Our bodies can never enter Truth, only our minds can! To
accomplish this, we need to learn the ways of communicating only the credible and veracious. When our hearts
begin to sing as one, all illusions of separation will rapidly

melt away. Extending peaceful, happy and altruistic thoughts of love, life, and healing, the Divine Will of our Creator will be known to us once more. Fully recognizing that His Power remains forever unopposed, our confidence and faith will only increase. As we eliminate all obstacles, our way becomes sure.

All outer unhappiness pictured on the screen of the world just reflects our inner turmoil and despondency. All insanity, chaos, and brutality we see, mirrors what remains broken within. The fault-line exists deep in our minds and thought, and there alone lies our place of salvation. Not comprehending this, we continue to wander lost and confused in an hostile and alien landscape. Thus we hoard worthless trinkets as our chosen means to salvation while living off any tiny scraps of pleasure we can plunder from the dream.

Our hearts have turned murderous as we eagerly fight to the death pursuing senseless ego ideals. Since thoughts of scarcity and loss continuously haunt and ravage our minds, we justify stealing all resources; we see of value. The vision that once was so natural and effortless has been clouded over by the blind eyes of judgment and condemnation. Judging that which we do not understand, we have lost the capacity to see the majestic Kingdom; that is before our very eyes. It has been rendered invisible by our calculating minds, narrow-minded thoughts and self-serving agendas.

This transmission is a course in both cause and cure. You will learn the deeper cause of all your unhappiness and the means to its alleviation. Slowly, it will dawn, on you, that this world is merely a symptom and not a cause in itself. Real cause lies far deeper and it needs to be successfully traced and resolved so that you can be awakened from the dream. In, **Part I,** of this series, the *Tiny-Mad-Idea* (**TMI**), I detailed how our '**Tiny-Mad-Idea**' (**TMI**) lead to our descent from our blissful state of divine unity. This catalytically triggered the loss of the Knowledge of Whole-Mind. Believing, we could successfully steal the power of our Creator, produced intense guilt. The greater part of this guilt lies so deeply buried within that we are mostly unconscious of it. In consequence, it is not registered in our active minds and thought. Nevertheless, its astronomical impact is still very much felt. This universe of separation arose from it, as did all our experiences of impermanence, fragility and of living in a body. We feel overwhelmed, at times, by the innumerable complexities of our existence and the impossible situation in which we are entangled.

In the previous teaching, I also briefly introduced **Learning Devices** and **Miracles of Forgiveness**. Both are essential spiritual tools, integral to our healing and release. The first phase of our fall into the Relative World began with our denial of our Father. The next phase was the emergence of this imaginary landscape of separation. Even though this world of our perception is entirely illusory; it can still feel compellingly real. It seems authenticated by all the deceptive information fed to us by our senses. Our exceedingly conditioned mindsets also serve to reinforce it. The very static, austere, object-orientated world we now perceive has crystallized from our inordinately fallacious beliefs.

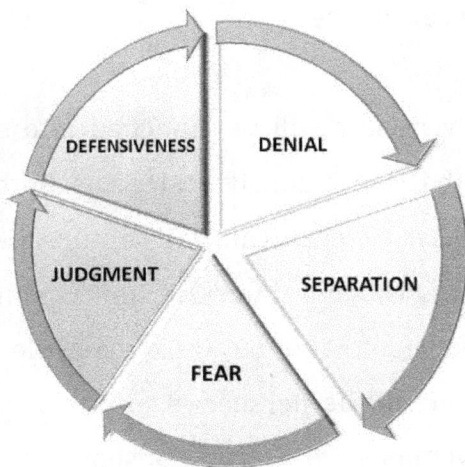

THE "VICIOUS" CAUSE-AND-EFFECT CYCLE THAT PERPETUATES THE RELATIVE WORLD

What would be most beneficial now, is intimately comprehending the profound implications, streaming from the
original error. We will begin by investigating how an os-
tensibly innocuous error can very rapidly and pervasively
proliferate. An ontological distinction will be drawn between the Absolute from the Relative so that you can
comprehend without any trace of ambiguity how the
thought system of the ego correlates with the Relative
World. The full dynamics by which the ego seeks to maintain itself in your thought will then be explored. In particular, the enduring connection between the ego and the dissociative condition, known as **"split-mind,"** will be exposed to light. Certain sacred cows of the ego will be laid
bare and debunked, including those myths of the body and
of objective existence.

A summary review will be launched into some everyday
problems that continuously besiege us, both at an individual and collective level. This will capture, very convincingly, how our problems interfuse and contagiously spread
from one form into another. Once the evidence is amassed,
I hope I you will be persuaded incontrovertibly, that all
worldly dilemmas are a direct consequence of our pseudo-
separation belief. A thorough analysis will then be initiated
into both the purpose and scope of learning devices. One,

which will outline their correct usage and the means to most efficaciously leverage them. As you progress, you will be gaining in spiritual vision and mystical insight. I will delve in detail into the learning devices of: **(i) The Body (ii) Spacetime** and **(iii) Consciousness and Perception**.

At this juncture, you may become more enthusiastic to implement the fundamental, (albeit subtle) inward shift demanded, to rapidly accelerate in your learning progress. Ready to engage, then, the evolutionary transformation in your conscious awareness, crucial to transcending the Relative Existence. Once you are released from all dualistic and split-mind modes of experiencing, the supra-conceptual realms will be increasingly present in your purview. One timeless instant is all it takes for a definite qualitative leap to occur in your awareness. Nonetheless, it will convince you of the tremendous influence and latent presence of these realms beyond all shadow of a doubt.

The diagram below overviews the *cause-and-effect* flow that brought us to where we seem to be now—a world of separation, in which we experience so many elaborate needs and where we feel perpetually lost and isolated. Since our experience of *Separation* is so compellingly real, it cannot be easily dismissed. Instead, we have become incredibly hypnotized by the dream we are living. The central learning devices which will enable us to escape this bleak manifold are thoroughly explored. As you may have gathered, an evolution in our consciousness is divinely mandated, before we can become reintegrated and healed. So do we finally vaporize and relinquish the mind-generated hallucination, that is the Relative World!

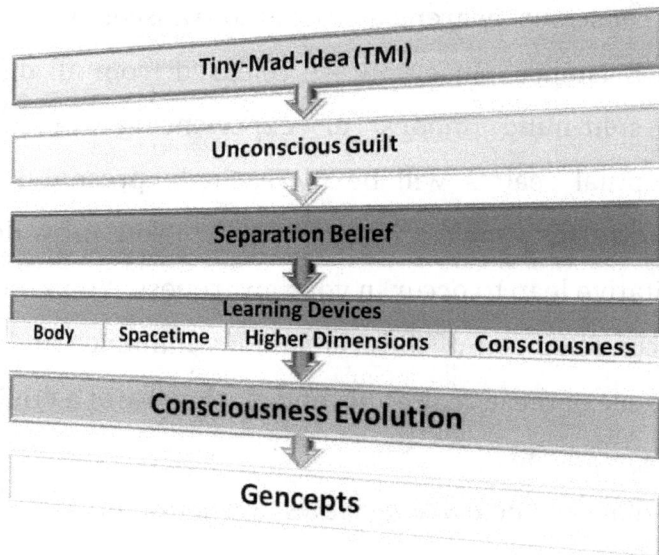

Tiny-Mad-Idea (TMI)			
Unconscious Guilt			
Separation Belief			
Learning Devices			
Body	Spacetime	Higher Dimensions	Consciousness
Consciousness Evolution			
Gencepts			

THE EFFECTS OF THE TMI AND THE EVOLUTIONARY PROGRESSION NEEDED TO ESCAPE THE WORLD

THE BEGINNING OF ERROR

(Sharon) This world of separation presents many serious problems. I doubt many would argue this point. Likewise, it can feel engagingly real, at times. **However, considering what a tangled mess it is, it seems sheer ludicrousness to conceive it all began with one wild thought.**

(Jesus) The *Tiny-Mad-Idea* was just the fatal trigger which set off the entire explosion. This introduced the original stain of impure thought into the mind. However the actual world of separation did not happen overnight but evolved gradually over millions of years, under the careful direction and neurotoxic massaging of your ego. All the same,, it remains an illusion, which began with a single error. Just as a woolen garment can be completed unraveled due a single tear. Likewise is it so with your entire descent into darkness. You may recall these words I spoke:

> **"You who believe that God is fear made but one**
>
> **substitution. It has taken many forms, because**
>
> **it was the substitution of illusion for truth; of**
>
> **fragmentation for wholeness. It has become so**

splintered and subdivided and divided again, over and over, that it is now almost impossible to perceive it once was one, and still is what it was. That one error, which brought truth to illusion, infinity to time, and life to death, was all you ever made. Your whole world rests upon it. Everything you see reflects it, and every special relationship that you ever made is part of it."

[ACIM, T-18.I.4:1-6]

(Sharon) Your illuminating words unquestionably pack some punch and make the overall picture abundantly clear! **I suspect we have all made some bad decisions, at times. Some, we never stop paying for!** Many marry the wrong person and are miserable ever after. Some repress their authentic identities; others their real passions. A number allow themselves to be badgered, manipulated and cajoled into doing something, they wholeheartedly disagree with and soon lose all sense of integrity. Peering back into the crystal ball of existence, the enormity of their one mistake can be too overwhelming to bear. However, the psychological glitch or faux pas often starts out decep-tively small, as to be almost invisible. Maybe the attraction was superficial, at first, and glaring red flags became con-veniently ignored. Red flags which soon compounded into gargantuan blunders, once one began living in intimate contact with the other, for an extended period. In conse-quence, the situation soon gravitated into a living hell.

Similarly, those who repress their real identities or pas-sions don't usually accomplish this all at once. Instead, their self-inflicted suicide happens slowly and day-by-day. Before they know it, entire decades have flown by, and they remain enmeshed in their frozen cocoons of amber, not living to their full capacities. They often rationalize each poor decision along the way, out of fear, ridicule or the need to pay the bills.

(Jesus) Definitely, no flies on you! However, many still find it hard to accept that a single error in decision, is entirely responsible for the insane world they now perceive. All the same, nothing has been the same since we the Sonship made that momentous mistake of thinking the *Tiny-Mad-Idea* (**TMI**). Though now long forgotten, its impact is still very much felt, and its devastating consequences are wit-nessed from every angle. This one idle thought substituted heaven with hell, eternity with spacetime and love with fear. It brought us to our knees and truly humbled us, in every sense. We, who but knew ourselves, only as perfect creations in the Kingdom of light now seem more like outright imbeciles and deeply fragmented souls. Before that mental and spiritual apocalypse, the world of death, suffering, and loss were entirely inconceivable. Now each experiences their existence through the distortionary prism of split-mind.

That error gave birth to both consciousness and perception, as well as to the world of bodies, diseases, and endless conflicts. It presented a world of a gazillion different devices, medical "cures," pills, patches, and addictions. One in which magical beliefs are rampant and thoughts of scarcity, attack and vengeance are on everyone's radar. Yes, much that is insidious has infused its way into the nexus of our thought and a dark veil has formed over our minds as our shield against the light. Within this tenebrous mushroom cloud, we each experience extensive anguish, confusion, injustice, and isolation. It has evolved, over time, into so many collective forms of pain including wars, genocides, political struggles, and numerous other mindless atrocities. We have become like colonies of ants dragging our toxic scent everywhere. Each, contaminating everyone else with their unique brand of sickness and unhinged behavior.

It has very much shaped our world and the toys we play with. The worlds of technology, invention, consumerism, espionage, cyber-wars etc. all arose, as our chosen dream substitutes for Creation. What a low-spirited convoluted world was heralded in, at that inglorious moment! A world, powered by so many deceptive forms of targeted marketing and e-conduits for misinformation propagation. A world of electronic combat and bit-banging tunnels in which e-media mobs head off on their cyber-lynching campaigns. It is all an online riot, just like the streets of LA, only far more treacherous, sneaky and recursively viral in its calamitous effects. Trojan click traps are everywhere ready to pounce and take us for every penny we have got. Yes, the single error caused all the damage, just as a missing gasket from a car can cause it to overheat and render it inoperative. It alone, had the power and capacity to dispossess perfect Knowledge from our awareness.

Thus each plods joylessly about through a veritable minefield of illusions feeling endlessly besieged by irresolvable contradictions and an infinite well of spiritual emptiness. All is an infernal ghetto, in which all prospects of clarity and hope seem irretrievably lost. With the departure of vision, we entered a sunless saturnine existence in which there is no longer any loving connection. Just this ambiguous gray hall of mirrors, where uncertainty and alienation rule the day. It is a real shark tank, in which each futilely gropes for any last straw of their sanity. However, analyzing darkness, guarantees blindness, just as uncovering correct understandings restores vision. Unfortunately, those who insist on invoking the powers of darkness as their guru will not escape the inevitable consequences of their misplaced loyalty. Remember these words, I spoke:

"Do not seek vision through your eyes, for you have made your way of seeing that you might see in darkness, and in this you are deceived. Beyond this darkness and yet still within you, is the vision of Christ, Who looks on all in light. Your "vision" comes from fear, as His from love."

[ACIM, T-13.V:9.1-3]

(Sharon) So where is our sanity and hope, to be found in all this?

(Jesus) As I have said, *"Inward is sanity; insanity is outside you."* [ACIM, T-18.I.7:4] Truth has always been present, silently waiting for you to reclaim it. However, the ego does not want you to go there and so it engages you in chasing ten thousand meaningless distractions. Distractions that include various pleasure-seeking games, infatuations, and obsessions with the body. Preoccupations with new inventions, and all those charades aimed at increasing your self-worth, image, and prestige in the eyes of the world. For time, is the terra-firma of the ego and it will never tolerate your entering the vertical dimension of the present. After millions of years swimming around in this luniverse, most have become blinded and hypnotized by the world of form. They continuously feast their eyes, on all that is without, and have long abandoned the search for the timeless and pure. The shadows on their cave wall, soak up all their attention. They do not seek that subtle, extremely potent, mystical essence, which alone can heal. Since the matrix of their perceptions crystallizes from all their judgments, conceptualizations, preferences, and tastes, they feel existentially pressured to play out their usual roles in this Dantesque tragedy. Thus they travel, for innumerable lives, making no major progress. Instead, each life spent in this joyless asylum, burns them up just a little more, chasing its transient toys and skin-deep pleasures.

Realize, then, that you are now so accustomed to seeing your way in darkness; that vision seems like a remote and intangible dream. Nevertheless, reality remains undiminished, even when obscured by all your foolish fantasies, incorrigible beliefs and general state of confusion. It can only be revealed through vision and holiness and is guaranteed to rise back into your awareness; once all your erroneous beliefs have been dispelled. The single error blitzed your mind with unsubstantiated guilt and this alone bars your release. Once conceived, it soon proliferated to leave no aspect of your thought or perception unaffected. It is just like a bacterium or virus that can grow asymptotically into colonies of billions, leading swiftly to new diseases and the demise of millions. After an extensive period, one could be considered crazy for believing a single thought could unleash such catastrophic effects. Mesmerized, conditioned and hypnotized by the worldly dream, one becomes mentally eclipsed to all advanced spiritual and teleological perspectives. Too shortsighted and myopic, therefore, to divine the exact root cause any longer. In fact, it now seems so trivial when compared to all the devastation wrought. In this sense, Truth can often seem stranger than fiction.

The original error of the TMI was the fountainhead through which all illusions poured. It is the belief that we can create powerful Kingdoms, in the absence of our Creator and it cogently reflects, the nonsensical ideation that our invented dream images can be made satisfying and whole and replace the truth, of who we Are! From this arose all meaningless effects showing up in our perception. Identifying with this overly distorted picture, we feel so uncertain and lost that we mistakenly believe our illusory kingdom is Reality. Nevertheless, it represents, an unshared thought, since God could never have contemplated it. It is thus uncreative and can never produce any real effects. This understanding is vital to finding your freedom. You can quietly and effectively relinquish all illusions by correcting those pernicious thought patterns, which silently produce them.

Like thieves in the night, we had sought to take everything for ourselves. To accomplish a coup d'état of God's power and be sovereign rulers in our private worlds. Even so, all we have built are joyless kingdoms in virtual reality. Ones, in which we feel supremely powerless and vulnerable. We cannot even enjoy a single moment's peace, without feeling intensely victimized by the haunting effects of our miscreative thought. Thus we roam about as diminutive Avatars in a dream. Grotesque creatures, with deathray eyes and flailing limbs, resembling nothing more than pitiful piles of extortionist dust on psycho-planet. We indulge endlessly, in very exclusive games of pulp fiction while feeling mercilessly hounded by the dream's strange powers. We paint smiley faces over our deep state of sadness, torment, and pain. Anxiety, insecurity, and fear have threaded their way acutely into our bones, paralyzing us to this human jungle; we cannot even fathom. The toxic ego chattering ringing in our ears makes it impossible for us to think straight. Dazed and confused, we are unable to ask any penetrating questions, anymore. Hence, we remain perpetually confused about ourselves. Nor can the ego, ever come to our rescue since it is incapable of Knowledge and has no revelatory answers to share. As I have said:

"The ego is the questioning aspect of the post-separation self, which was made rather than created. It is capable of asking questions but not of perceiving meaningful answers, because

these would involve knowledge and cannot be

perceived."

[ACIM, T-3.IV.3:1-2]

"Errors are of the ego, and correction of errors

lies in the relinquishment of the ego."

[ACIM, T-9.III.2:3]

Viewed from the microcosm of your personal life, perhaps you have insight, into how a single mistake can often pro-create and soon prove fatal. An error in thought can dark-en your entire world and have a multiplicity of conse-quences downstream; that seem totally unrelated to the original incident. So it is with the twisted and tortuously anfractuous realm, you now perceive! It all arose from very humble beginnings. Nevertheless, all forms of sickness, depression, substance abuse, suicide, and murder derive from our continued collective belief in separation. And what causes the belief in separation, but the belief in guilt! The relatively minor and laughable mistake, of the **TMI**, which brought about our entire fall from grace has com-pounded in its effects in the millions of years of illusory time since.

You may recall the movie *"The Deer Hunter"* from the '70s, in which the lead actor, Mike Vronsky (Robert De Niro) is so adamant in his insistence *"One Bullet! One Deer."* God's plan of salvation is very similar because we all made but a single mistake, and this requires a single solution. The *Tiny Mad Idea* triggered guilt thoughts to flood our minds and a world of separation to emerge. All the same, our belief in guilt can be completely cured through quantum for-giveness. This is the magic bullet that eradicates the ego and all guilt-based beliefs. The power of forgiveness is in-contestable to a loving, and devoted mind because when-ever you truly forgive another, you cannot be attacking, judging or condemning them. Nor will you see them, then, as sinful and beyond reproach. Instead, you will have come to awareness of your far greater unity. Increased integra-tion with your True Identity, is what heals.

Many spiritual teachers, healers, and psychiatrists have emphasized the ego as the entire cause of all our problems. They are correct! The ego, though a fictional entity, is cer-tainly a headache without a head. The complete myth of its existence is fabricated out of our beliefs. We do not pos-sess an ego, so much as we are hypnotized and manipulat-ed by its mere conception. How can one cure a headache, if one cannot find the head? The only hope is to undo your belief there ever was a head. As I mentioned many times, the Holy Spirit is your guide on this. He can quickly release all unsound beliefs and all that is unwisely cherished. He can annihilate the ego and vaporize it from your thought.

All problems in the relative world are entirely fictitious. They are generated out of lethal and deleterious ego thinking strategies and the inevitable knee-jerk reactions. However, the ego being unreal, does not lend itself to direct frontal assault. Like all forms of darkness, it can never be expunged, through increased analysis. In fact, the more one tries to make sense out of the ego, the more one falls into its dark pits. Affirming its divisive rhetoric and insane rackets is how it grows and becomes empowered. It only loses its power and traction in your mind, to the extent that you become willing to connect with the Spirit in all. When you emphasize and assert exclusively only the sanity in another, you heal the illusory split in the Mind; you both share. Not knowing this Mind and its wisdom, is the source of all your pain and confusion.

"The study of the ego is not the study of the mind. In fact, the ego enjoys studying itself, and thoroughly approves the undertakings of

students who would "analyze" it, thus approving its importance. Yet they but study form with meaningless content. For their teacher is senseless, though careful to conceal this fact behind impressive sounding words, but which lack any consistent sense when they are put together."

[ACIM, T-14.X.8:6-9]

You may believe, I am the voice of your ego and that this communication is only empty ego hot air abounding in useless metaphors and hyperbolic language. Does this seem likely? If you are only hearing me through your ego, that is exactly what you will believe. In fact, this is the complete healing message! Because you are always hearing, seeing, interpreting and understanding based on your present mindstate. Your mindset does not exist in a vacuum but derives its fuel from all your motives, desires and intentions. These determine who you place at the controls. So who have you presently empowered at your helm? The ego or the Voice of God? Your answer to this is crucial to your continued progress and attainment of Peace.

One should never undertake a study of the ego lightly or without stealth and caution. The ego likes to vacillate, rationalize, procrastinate and play all sorts of wicked games in your mind. Unless you administer the cure, nothing will ever get accomplished. To the extent that you introduce the light, the darkness naturally disappears. One cannot shine away darkness through analysis, no matter how long one spends. The ego's pseudo-existence depends entirely on the absence of light.

From the instant of the seeming fall, most of your thoughts and energies have been consumed licensing and sanctioning the unreal. Your blind certification of the world of appearances has blocked your awareness of Truth. Your mind now seems split because of the presence of both the ego and Holy Spirit in it. Both their belief systems, you only partially endorse. Both are consistent, but diametrically opposed. Only the Holy Spirit's however, exists in light and reflects Knowledge. When you affirm only the Holy Spirit's Thought, will you be released to the wisdom of Whole-Mind.

Meanwhile, the ego surrounds itself with a very imposing and labyrinthine network of defense. One that has evolved into a veritable empire and fortress since the instant of the seeming fall. One so vast and complex, that you no longer remember where the halls of merriment and court jesters are—only the dungeons. Heeding its counsel out of fear brainwashes you into adopting its hopeless defensive strategies as your safety and protection. This presents a scary place to your senses, for it aims to distort all truth into untruth. It is this intricate array of armaments, closed doors, and whispering corridors which alone maintain and reinforce your belief in separation.

The safety and protection of a wave lie in its unity with the ocean. All its meaning derives from its seamless unification with that which is far more powerful than itself. Apart, it can be quickly evaporated by the sun. It has no function alone and stands entirely meaningless. Likewise, once you dissolve back into the ocean of the One-Mind, all that is strange, extraneous and conflicting will disappear from your thought. Your understanding will become perfect, and your perception run crystal clear. This merging with the ocean will wipe out all that is false and inherited. Knowledge is already yours, but this wisdom remains shrouded by your ego distortions. Once you relinquish the ego, you will regain direct vision of the Eternal paradise, where you have always been.

UNIVERSAL TRUTH IS

(Sharon) Is Truth Absolute or Relative? What are some of the obstacles that prevent us from witnessing it?

(Jesus) Truth is most assuredly Absolute. If it were relative, it would be conditional and therefore subject to changes in external conditions and belief adjustments in your mind. Truth must remain forever beyond all your beliefs and conditionings because these fluctuate, all too readily. Changing your beliefs is the means to uncover Truth. However, beliefs are powerless to produce it. All beliefs lack your complete faith and confidence, or there would be certitude. Once your understanding is correct, Truth will reveal itself. Incorrect beliefs, in contrast, distort your view and cover Reality with a dark obfuscating mantle.

Universal truth already exists complete deep inside your mind. It is only your attraction to ignorance that prevents you from voyaging there.

The Knowledge of Spirit is your link to Truth, but because you choose the ego, you remain dispirited. Your firm conviction in false beliefs establishes an inner inertia to progress; collectively known as ignorance. Such beliefs inter-pose themselves as a shadowy veil over Truth and taken together are synonymous with the ego. The ego represents nothing more than your pitiful attempts at self-validation through cherishing foolish attachments, petty vengeful-ness, and shallow desires. Such are your ego's chosen re-placements for God and His Kingdom. All illusions arise through ego-investments, and the ego remains nothing more than a mirage appearing out of your chosen distor-tionary beliefs.

You have never been separate from the all-encompassing unity of the Kingdom and only in this Holy immersion, can you be known once more. This awareness is the ultimate form of Self-validation since it restores the Knowledge of your divine Creation. All ego attempts at validation amount to nothing more than appending a maze of pretentious il-lusions, to that which is already flawless and pure. Asking which came first, the ego or the separation is utterly mean-ingless because both are interdependent and reinforce one another. When the ego and its thought is finally relin-quished, the apparent separation will be no more. Igno-rance, the birth of illusion, and the ego are all simultane-ous. They can be said to be interdependently co-arising. The more you are not in tune with Universal Truth, the more the pseudo-reality of the ego grows — just like the bird in the Zen Master's bottle. Nursing your continued ego wishes to think apart, you begin to feel increasingly alienated and disconnected. So you become inhibited from freely using all the creative energy which is your divine inheritance. The ego can never amount to anything more than a halo of smoke, for which there is no fire. This halo of smoke is like a perpetual flimflam man that tap-dances on the surface of your mind. One that is circumference everywhere and center nowhere. Truth, in contradistinction, is center everywhere and circumference nowhere.

Most allow themselves to become band-limited to ridiculous ego beliefs which then quickly transmogrify into chains and manacles that bind. Mental chains that shape their lives and legacies and determine the nature of their self-made hells. Outside, they go about with the painted smiles of happiness and continually alternate between one mask and the next. All in a vain and futile attempt to demonstrate their completion. Inwardly their spirits are screaming in anguish. Spirit just wants to go Home. It no longer desires to be tied, like a giant elephant to the stick of their egos. But their personal devil must be appeased whatever the cost. So they remain confined in the animal arena, nourishing a host of base resentments and open hostilities while paying homage to their god of nothing-ness.

You can, however, break completely free of the ego, any-time and for good. One sincere effort is all it takes to snap free of its crippling hold. Then the sickness that pervades your mind will be fumigated out of existence. No complex system of mental calisthenics is required—only honesty, simplicity, and genuine humility. A little willingness on your part to recognize all appearances outside are not sep-arate from your thoughts. The world is just an image in form; that cogently reflects all your strange desires and lifeless thoughts. A mirror for the murky pool of your mind. Once you choose, only what is worthy, this pool transforms into a limpid and rejuvenating oasis. Then you get a full swig of your perennial freedom.

The ego is that troublesome, irritating monkey on your back who so often causes your blood to boil. Now is the moment to take that hollow-point to its coconut and set yourself free of all inner demons. Yes jump on its back, yelling "*Yee-haw*" and ride it to the rails. Let now be your moment to shine, in a life otherwise filled with mediocrity. Powerful and transformative change is but a thought away. Meaningful purpose follows from sincere listening. You only find this difficult because you have become so tarnished and corrupted by impure ego motives. Your capitulation, for instance, to various superficial desires, illicit temptations, guilt based thoughts and certain quixotic misadventures which serve no useful purpose. However, one real thought has sufficient potency to transform your entire world experience. Once you allow it to gain unconscious traction, appeal, and momentum, it will automatically direct all your subsequent thoughts, actions, and behaviors. It will accumulate all that is in its likeness until your entire perception is transfigured into a stunning portrait of radiance.

Uncertainty, is the path to wisdom, just as certainty leads to blindness. The ego enjoys holding you hostage to states of mental distraction. Thus, it curses your true perceptions and suffocates your life. Similarly, it handicaps through various mental filters and imprisoning beliefs. Only when you despair of all its offerings and recognize their underlying emptiness, can the dark seal of egoic thought finally be broken. Then its game is up and its once boisterous ranting diminishes to a whisper.

All who come to Truth must pass through despair because despair is the healing touchstone which exposes the ego and opens your eyes.

The ego will abandon the house once despair arrives as your guest. It is terrified to find out what is on the other side of this door. Despair works through bringing a sudden stop to your dream machine. It halts your mind's conditioned tendencies to continuously hallucinate and project. It ferries you into the true present where you no longer project future dreams or take malicious vengeance on your past. So do, you enter a passive state of blank unknowingness.

It is on this blank canvas that Truth can, at last, be written. When your mind reaches a state of unobstructed readiness, the divine automatically enters. Where no illusions are cherished, Truth comes gratefully on its own.

(Sharon) This all reminds me of a poem I once wrote, called *Time Betrayal*. It seems time and the ego have a lot in common. Both entice us to follow their paths with blind loyalty and then abandon us at the moment of our greatest need.

TIME BETRAYAL

I

One day, I decided to follow Time!

I followed it through Day,

Night, Hardship and

Difficulties!

I followed it through Loneliness,

Sickness, Poverty, and Fear!

I even followed it,

During Blackouts and,

Moments of Insanity!

II

My Mind became Hazy,

Lifeless and Dull!

Even So, I kept Persisting,

Out of Habit, I Suppose!

Time showed me the Loves,

Passions, and Joys of my Life!

But was Forever Insistent

to Move On!

During the Good Times,

Time Moved Faster!

During the Bad Times,

Slower!

III

Gradually I Began,

to Despise Time!

But kept on Following,

For it had Become,

The Measure of Me,

I even Plotted my Life,

along its Markers!

Then one Fatal Day,

Time brought me to

Hell on Earth,

and said

" I'll be off, Now!

and Don't know,

if I'll be Back! "

IV

I felt so Letdown

and Angrily Vociferated,

"How can you do This?

After all my Loyalty

to you,

Over the Years?"

At that Exact Moment,

"The Instant"

Kindly Tapped Me,

on the Shoulder,

and Said

"Follow me Instead!

For I will take you Home!

Forget all about,

That Lying, Sneaky, Thieving,

and Deceiving Bastard!"

THE INUIT

HEADING OFF ON THE ICE-PACK

(Jesus) The Inuit, when advanced in age and no longer able to nourish or support themselves, often simply wander off on the ice-pack to die. You may think, they have reached the point of absolute despair, doing such an act, but in fact, their situation runs completely antipodal to the ego. Theirs is a celebration of life and existence. One of having lived fully while enjoying many beautiful experiences. Now having given all and treasured much, they have reached the tacit inner realization that the purpose of this particular lifecycle is over.

Tremendously satisfied, grateful and at peace, they recognize their future is all used up. Nor do they wish, to become an unnecessary burden on others. So unselfishly they walk off and sacrifice their bodies as one last parting gift to nature. Thus they can continue on their spiritual progression in a newly rejuvenated form.

Our ice-packs come in many different varieties and forms. It can be in the desert, a forest or while at sea. An ice-pack will be anywhere where we willingly self-isolate ourselves or become detached from the greater stream of humanity, to meet our end.

(Sharon) Earlier today, I released a helium balloon that had become deflated from hanging around in my apartment for far too long. With its last residual dregs of pressurized air, it was able to soar high into the clear blue sky above and disappear from view. Thus it gained its freedom with its dying gasp of air and entered the Nirvana of Helium balloons. I think this was its ice-pack.

(Jesus) I guess that is one way of looking at it.

(Sharon) How will we recognize when we are ready for our ice-pack?

(Jesus) Those who live a full, adventurous and far-reaching life, who work tirelessly to attain to insight, wisdom, and even enlightenment will be ready for their ice-pack when it comes. Lao Tzu's last act in life, before walking off on to his ice-pack of Mongolia was to pour all his wisdom into the profound spiritual teaching, known as *Tao-Te-Ching*. This fountain of his inner wisdom became the very foundation for Taoism. He was ready for his ice-pack, even though it came in the form of a desert.

The ego's despair has an entirely different quality. It arises from holding too many unreasonable demands and conflicting desires. It is forever overburdened with dreams of specialness and conquest and is at perpetual war with the world around it. How can such a mindstate, ever hope to gain lasting peace and happiness? Since it is one that is incessantly pestering, controlling and extorting all. The ego is always placing you in an impossible situation. One, in which you are doomed to fail from the start. It continually projects the source of all pain to an "external" world, rather than recognize its inner emptiness and lack of noble purpose. All its existential recipes lead to your ultimate despair. You must, therefore, learn how to relinquish the ego, as you gave birth to it. This important step places you on the path towards Truth. As you build strength and spiritual energy, you will find you are no longer clutching idly at its futile straws and pipe dreams but progressing steadily on the sure path to happiness. It continually projects the source of all pain to an "external" world, rather than recognize its inner emptiness and lack of noble purpose.

THE EGO DEMYSTIFIED

(Sharon) The ego and our beliefs in separation seem to go hand-in-hand. **So what is the ego's game-plan and what are the full dynamics by which it gains an upper hold in our minds?**

(Jesus) The ego aims to keep you hostage to a ragged and exhausting depot. A corrosive and cynical world of primal gratifications etched on a screen of abiding misery. One in which a sickening triumvirate of desire, fear, and doubt prevail from every direction and where each hunts for any tiny scraps of pleasure they can rescue from the garbage dumps of our lives!

So you travel through the mists of a disenchanted waste-land, busy working on contingency plans for problems that may never arise. Your mind is so doggedly rooted in future time that you cannot even claim happiness when it comes your way. Instead, you take all for granted and quickly pass by those newly blossomed flowers, that sparkle with luster and iridescence under the fresh morning dew. Each life, when reviewed, is but a series of pointless energy expenditures and dilemmas carefully manufactured by the ego to deflect from living totally in the present.

One of the greatest problems is that each worships only their ego's notions of success. Most are self-sabotaging beings with no foolproof plan, purposeful direction or inner fire. They lack the well-primed intention, incorrigible will, and necessary follow-through. Their goals are as whimsical and superficial, as they are contradictory and poorly formulated. They have lost all vision to peer beyond the pale of their tiny worldly cubbyholes. Hence they wander aimlessly about, feeling thoroughly worn down by all the minutiae of life. Feeling unremittingly victimized by meaningless project schedules and tiresome inter-office politics. Consumed by the process of getting a paycheck and seeking more rags to garment in glory their scaffolding of flesh and bone.

In desperation, each voraciously seeks out all forms of external validation and eagerly soaks up any tiny morsels of attention they can garner for all their beliefs, accomplishments, and nonsense opinions. Likewise, they craftily exploit all forms of ingenuity, guile, and deception to present illusions of their power. Viscerally pouncing on all those ad hoc groups and societies that make them feel privileged while stealthily avoiding all those awkward, uncomfortable folk who have the power to burst their bubble.

They hope one day to escape all these toxic environments, where they feel only barely alive. Perhaps they can steal a few Kodak moments and indulge in a few of life's basic pleasures before finally kicking the bucket. Naturally, they relentlessly ignore their heart's deeper ambitions because they are too fearful to dip below the horizon and venture into that nebulous underworld. Thus they cling tenaciously to those superficial trappings of success presented only at the surface and settle for the package instead of the gift.

The result is inevitable. Each morphs rapidly into an overly conditioned being. One too spineless to stick out and be their authentic self. All quickly rationalize the gross and subtle psychological tortures they have unwittingly invited into their lives, if it will only help them save face, one more day. The next picture is of an old, tired, tattered and broken down body enjoying his last sunset while greedily guzzling oxygen from the tank next to his wheelchair.

To each, their own personal flavor of madness and eccentricity. For most, it will be a lifetime of procrastination and chronic absorption in meaningless activities. One in which the body becomes progressively deified and faithfully pandered to for all its needs. Consequently each takes great pains to give it all the food, exercise, medical care, security and comfort it needs. Even still, it disintegrates before your very eyes. Hence this once great carnival of flesh and the bonfire of all passions is soon transformed into a very sickly portraiture, that reflects your own Dorian Gray! One that convincingly reveals in all its wrinkles, sockets and hollowed out orifices the genuine resume of your weary and guilt-ridden life.

Yes, those death-rays shine from your soulless circular orbits preaching to all the tale of your snuffed-out inner hope. Your dry gaping mouths, desiccated by a lifetime of investment in greed can only expound now the foulest and wicked mutterings. So we hear the many demons of the tongue vomiting out their senseless vile gibberish in a furious cacophony of mind-grating wails. Yes your life will have no 4th of July moments. Instead your body's gradual deterioration will finally leave you as a sun-dried tomato on a parched existential desert. A wasteland devoid of any noteworthy achievement or any savoring grace. As for the mind, with each passing year, it will lessen in its vibrancy, clarity, acuity, and creative vision. An inertial force-field will set in to imbue it with those rascals of inflexibility and intransigence. It will become increasingly circumvented to all that is newly emergent. Then enter the death throes of psychological rigor-mortis, long before its capacities for memory retention are all wiped out. Yes, the external validation each craves becomes much more challenging as they proceed. One reaches a point of diminishing returns, in which all motivation becomes sacrificed to those old-time methuselahs of entropy and dissolution.

Younger generations will pay scant attention to the potent insights and greater wisdom that has crystallized within you, from a lifetime of experiences. No! they will want to screw things up royally in their own ingenious ways. Thus they too will be humbled and then outright humiliated. For the curse of the young is their blind trust, just as that of the old is their entire lack of it. Each starts out fresh as an incorrigible and hopeless idealist but soon converts into an incurable cynic. Each begins their life drama feeling existentially cushioned and invulnerable. Feeling protected by the powers that be until something fateful and tragic happens that forces them to face their mortality and limits.

All too soon your progeny will be coming to fetch you. Seeking to put you into a nursing home — that is if you are lucky enough. A plethora of expert doctors and psychotherapists will then arrive on the scene to diagnose you with a multiplicity of physical and mental diseases. Dazed and confused, you will hear so many strange sounding words whizzing by your ears and then witlessly walk out into the hail of bullets. Met with those authoritative, euphonic sounding words like hypertension, diabetes, gout, arrhythmia and stroke as well as a host of neurological disorders including Dementia, Alzheimer's, Parkinson's and ALS. Why not throw flatulence and halitosis into the bargain to complete the indignity? It is evident at this stage they just want to chemically bombard you into neuroleptic numbness and shock. Then they can close up shop. Any hope of your redemption is like waiting for a lifeboat while aboard the Titanic.

You will feel yourself drowning in the void of self-annihilation. Drowning under all those symptoms and ailments that have been projected to your body and mind. You have become nothing now but a sacrificial lamb for the new slaughterhouse of the capitalistic marketplace. A test pilot for the new drug regimes. Since there is a price tag also associated with your body, they will keep you alive, long after your death-wish has gone into overdrive.

(Sharon) Sounds like a pretty bleak picture and one in which the ego has set us up to fail. But is it true? It seems undeniable that the body appears to degenerate with time, so as to become a living tomb. Sometimes, I wonder whether our minds really lessen with time, or is it that the apparatus for our thought expression simply become non-functional? It certainly seems that an individual's core personality type, unique mode of living and underlying processes of thought do not change much with age.

It is evident, however, that a day soon arrives, when each scatters the idealism of their youth into the seven oceans! A point when they feel Truth is powerless to rescue them. Instead, it seems entirely impotent and ready to be declared post-mortem. Perhaps, we have killed it, you and I, while dancing on the voluptuous waves of pleasure, sensual delight, intoxication, and specialness. Likewise, we vanquish our hopes of healing in our interminable attraction to kill all that is not in our likeness.

(Jesus) Nonsense! There is no real place, where the ever-perfect and changeless can be transmuted into the valueless! No real place where the Son of God can be trampled upon or sullied. Only in an illusory kingdom of the mind, can this seem possible? As I said in the Course:

"The separation was not a loss of perfection,

but a failure in communication."

[ACIM, T-6.IV.12:5]

You cannot lose your original state of perfection — only your awareness of it. All appearances of separation and decaying bodies arise from lending your ears too freely to the ego. It is this mad minion alone that facilitates all breakdowns in real communication. It lures you in through various idols and dreams of specialness and power. So you fall witlessly into its snares and appear to roam about a psychotic-universe, feeling all alone and abandoned by God. But this is your choice, and you can just as easily decide otherwise and undo your complete nightmare.

Were you listening to and communicating with the Holy Spirit instead, you would have realized by now that all separation and change is an illusion. All that seems to change has always been non-existent, as is the body. There is no way for the Eternal to be subdued and overcome, anymore than storm clouds can come to quench the Sun.

Howl as the ego may, send all its thunder, lightning, and torrential downpours it likes; these represent nothing more than ephemeral vapor streams that can be easily shined away. The complete illusion of its existence rests on the faith, complicity and dedication your mind continuously extends to its delusional system of thought.

So Truth is only temporarily lost to your awareness, to the extent that you nourish ego beliefs and dreams. All illusions and all appearances arise out of its distortions. Likewise, the body and all visible changes wrought on it in time will be seen no more once Holy Vision is restored. Your hallucinatory experiences are not reality. They merely reflect what you choose to cling to and continue to endorse.

UNMASKING THE WORLDLY DECEPTION

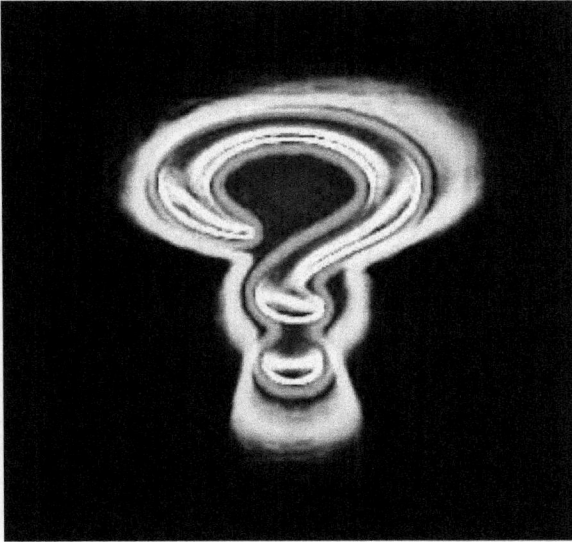

(Sharon) Is this world then nothing but a powerhouse of lies? Are all our conflicts, misunderstandings and persistent failures in communication producing a picture of extreme devastation?

(Jesus) Who can communicate nonsense meaningfully? Nevertheless, nonsense beliefs are embedded deeply into the very fabric of your society, at every level. You believe in a self-contained object-orientated universe. One built on the sacred cow of epiphenomenalism. This reversed basis amplifies judgment and fear. In consequence, endless hostilities and resentments simmer and seethe unchecked just below the surface! In it your mind is seen as weak, and subject to the arbitrary whims of the body! Is it a wonder then that you cave so readily to various magical beliefs and come to see your mind as an endangered species?

You rarely doubt the "wisdom" of your ego! Placing it at the helm, you rapidly lose all capacity for reason and meaningful questioning. Instead, living exclusively in this puffed-up cloud of smoke, you eagerly lap up all the empty, superficial ideologies and gossipy rhetoric circulated by the media.

Thus, lost in the mists of your deceitful persuasion, you can no longer penetrate anything to its core.

Severely tarnished by impure motives and false identifications you automatically become restricted to very narrow-banded agendas. Is it a surprise then that you find yourself suffocating under the perpetual haze of worldly complexities and lies?

Meaningful questioning has the power to transport you to unconditional peace. Such a noble pursuit is rendered powerless, however, if you insist on holding on to false, prejudiced and self-limiting beliefs. Its purpose after all, is to eliminate all impurities of thought so that you can effortlessly reach to perfect understanding. It must be obvious that all questions nourished in a barren context cannot bear fruit. Only by examining the very context itself, can wisdom be reached! Juggling beliefs born out of the sterile and lifeless cannot penetrate through to the real. Can a shadow point you to the glory of the sun?

THE EXPERIENCE OF SPLIT-MIND

(Sharon) You said before that each of us experiences our existence here through the distortionary prism of split-mind. **What is split-mind and what is its relationship to our beliefs in separation?**

(Jesus) The relative world, imposing though it may seem, can only be witnessed by a mind that is profoundly split. There has never been any world apart from its thinker. All that is perceived just faithfully reflects the composite of your beliefs.

Your mind became sundered the moment it entertained the original error. This caused a large-scale ruction within and from then on both truth and untruth seem to be waging war. All that you rejected seems to appear outside, in the landscape of your perception. Nevertheless, this is an illusion and you have merely dissociated from aspects of your own thought. The inevitable result is you now perceive a world, in which everything invariably wears out, fails or disintegrates and one whose deeper meaning is anything but evident. Nonetheless, this screen, you see is not the maker of its own light. It merely reflects your current state of consciousness. Without the light of consciousness, nothing would be seen. Perceiver and perceived are two dualistic aspects of one greater whole. Both are phantoms that disappear once the purity of Whole-Mind is known. Whole-Mind alone can know because it transcends objective / subjective duality. Not apprehending this, you remain trapped in the dream of duality. So you enter the guise of a particular personality type and seem to function as a separate self. In contrast, those who transcend are aware only of the Absolute and the immeasurable potency of pure Being.

Your Real Self is not conscious because consciousness always implies a mode of dualistic experiencing. Consciousness is synonymous with the ego and the domain of split-mind. In your enduring haze of impurity, you can easily entertain illusions as Reality. What IS, on the other hand, cannot be conceived or perceived because it transcends all conception and perception. It will always remain unknown by those who experience the relative world because it has no phenomenal existence whatsoever. Nonetheless, it is the eternal substratum from which all is derived, and all phenomenal appearances are contingent on it. When phenomenalism appears, it seems to disappear. Phenomenal experiencing is an impure mode of Being while Creation derives from a pure state of knowing.

The world of perception remains forever passive and has no power to do. There is no way for a man's shadow to become the man. All perceptions reflect only your inner movements of thought. They are the spontaneous outcome of all your understandings and beliefs. The relative world has no intrinsic Laws by which it operates, apart from those mentally projected to it. As you your Self-understanding grows, the world of perception glows with your newfound Vision.

The being, of separate beings, Is non-separated

Being.

[Chuang-Tse]

Your beliefs shape your conceptual understandings and become projected outwards as images you then relate to. All forms, percepts and phenomena you perceive arise from your "split" mind. These determine your entire world experience. Whenever your beliefs are incorrect, your conceptual understandings will lack light and lose alignment to Truth. The impact is mental contraction, confusion, sickness, and depression. The good news is your split-mind is an illusion generated out of wrong beliefs. Even so, what are these beliefs, except ego allegiances. The healing of this illusory mode of experiencing is the work of Salvation. The principal danger is becoming overly identified and hypnotized by this world of appearances and so forgetting you made the whole show up. It is a severe mistake to take what you see to be an actuality, instead of a mere reflection in a mirror.

Unfortunately, one's manifold identifications and attachments can keep one fast asleep. So you become a seeming prisoner of your mental constructs and erroneous beliefs and spend your days judging, sorting and classifying the unreal. Amplifying that which you like and rejecting/ignoring all else. Since judgment fragments and distorts, the whole seems discombobulated into separate parts. Parts that no longer seem to carry any meaningful relationship to the whole. Meaning can only be known when the complete picture is seen. Each part taken in isolation is meaningless.

For example, suppose we were to shred Vincent Van Gogh's painting "Starry Night" into a million different pieces. Suddenly we are left with a big pile of refuse. We can spend the rest of our lives studying this montage of paper-mâché and yet fail to see the beauty and meaning inherent in the original. None of the parts taken in isolation can point to it. Unless they are reassembled, the emotion, inspiration, and charm behind the original seem lost.

Our experience of split-mind became projected outward as a world of separation. This dissociated condition known as split-mind needs healing before one can transcend the realm of error. Until then, each continues to perceive a relative world of spacetime, which is but a mirage of their own false dualistic understandings. Quantum Forgiveness is the remedy needed to heal this dissociation because it functions to unify all that is real while purging all else. Relinquishing judgment and divisiveness, it enables one's true Identity to shine. Each, therefore, must take the important step of recognizing the world of separation is nothing but an illusory end-product of their own split-mind. This false picture alone stands as a barrier to Truth.

PROBLEMS ARISING FROM
THE SEPARATION

(Jesus) All problems can be broken down into four main categories.

1. **Small problems at the Individual level**

2. **Large problems at the Individual level**

3. **Small problems at the Collective level**

4. **Large problems at the Collective level**

LARGE, INDIVIDUAL
- Death of a Child
- Starvation
- Cancer
- A Year Spent in Solitary Confinement

LARGE, COLLECTIVE
- War
- Pandemics
- Genocide
- Total Environmental Destruction

PROBLEMS OF SEPARATION

SMALL, INDIVIDUAL
- A Broken Toe-Nail
- Nasty Boss
- Coffee Spilled on Sofa
- Insomnia

SMALL, COLLECTIVE
- International Soccer Defeat
- Flu Epidemic
- Stock Market Fluctuation
- Panic at a Shopping Sale

THE PROBLEMS OF SEPARATION

This partitioning of problems is somewhat arbitrary and not very illuminating in itself. All the same, what many do not recognize is that small problems at the individual level can soon ripple to become major problems at the collective level. Patient Zero, is one prime example. He seemed to have a minor ailment, but it soon spread its contagion to become the global HIV crisis. Even a broken toe-nail can agitate and distract one long enough so as to create a multi-car pile-up on the highway. Thus compounding into many fatalities and broken lives.

Similarly, one man's greed may trigger a commodity sell-off in the stock market, leading to tribal warfare in a remote country that is the sole supplier of that resource. The knock-on effect of this may be tens of thousands of migrating refugees, famine, contaminated water supplies, and new strains of a virus propagating globally. Likewise, the hate or prejudice of one individual can soon spread its insidious influence to multitudes. Malicious rumors and humor can often work in much the same way. A well-established comedian, who insists on leveraging his career off religious jokes may soon polarize entire groups, leading to the persecution of minorities.

(Sharon) You could include writers in that category. It is still fresh in my mind, the intense atmosphere and sense of outrage created when Salman Rushdie first published his *"Satanic Verses."* These days, we see an entirely new debate arising. One particularizing the limits and scope to which freedom of information and speech should be extended. WikiLeaks had a large-scale impact, and yet this was primarily the brainchild of one individual.

(Jesus) Freedom of speech and expression has always been an illusion in any civilization. Remember, I had only good things to say, and still they crucified me. Anytime you wander outside the accepted "norms," bad things can happen. Try living as openly LGBT in some middle-eastern country. Then run for political office and see how far you can go.

You can easily test your freedom for yourself. Simply go roaring and cursing through your neighborhood, late at night while running around naked. See how long it is before you are thrown into jail or evicted. Perhaps, if you trek into the desert or to the Artic, you can still exercise some freedom of speech without encountering too much dissent or animosity. But then maybe even the snakes and polar bears will get pissed off with you before long.

(Sharon) Yes, the "norms" are always changing from one time-period to another and from one culture to the next. Pederasty, for example, was a perfectly acceptable practice in Ancient Greece but nowadays it can easily land you a few decades behind bars wearing those glorifying orange and red jumpsuits of the crazed Gorilla.

In recent years, I have witnessed the corporate regression back to the slave ownership model. Overnight, our institutions have become twisted into human molding machines and excessively sanitized organizations. Yes, the stern atavistic backslide into stifling, politically correct institutions seems currently *en vogue*. All they want now is to print out these servile gingerbread men in stacks and wads. Extreme vigilance is demanded to live in these suffocating microcultures. Nano-managers are constantly hotfooting it about, waving their whips in the air, trying to squeeze an extra ounce of productivity out of their designated drudges. All amid that stupefying scent of sweat, stress, and blood.

One needs to be very cautious of every word spoken, and of any unintended nuance or e-mail sent. We are all walking on eggshells and tremendously afraid to offer our valuable input, just in case it may be labeled as confrontational or strike at someone's sensitivities. None remain, who will dare tell the emperor, he is wearing no clothes. There is too much fear of civil prosecution or of being booted out.

In milder cases, whenever one raises honest and critical objections, they can be quickly labeled pig-headed and ostracized from the group. Then penalized in performance reviews or outright fired. Then if you dare to run amok with HR, no amount of scrying into the crystal ball is going to save you. I think many of us have experienced this. Corporations say they want the brightest and best, but they seem totally unable to respond to healthy confrontation, despite its ramifications for positively transforming the very nature of their business. All they really want now are those meek malleable flatfish who will execute all their nonsense tasks, without ever posing any illuminating questions or demonstrating any critical thinking. So the dregs that remain is a bleak mind-numbing cocktail indeed. One consisting of those brownnosing drones, primadonnas, and utterly unimaginative types, who are just there to milk a paycheck and say *"Yes, Mister Miyagi."*

Most detestable of all are those silent effete limp-wristed enablers. The lamblike emasculated ones who have capitulated to the insatiable demands of the corporate oligarchical dictatorship. Cowards to the bone, that have let the enemy in to run its ruse — like the French in WWII. So we all feel existentially pressured to work around the clock like battery operated minions. Condemned to be passively non-resistant, to the hand of an evil empire. Thus it is given a carte blanche to steal away all vestiges of our hobbies, interests, home life and any semblance of normality. These are the treasured ones, those golden boys, and girls, prodigal sons, and daughters, who will always go above and beyond the call of duty. Those entrusted with the keys of the kingdom and the gatekeepers who will reprimand. Don't you dare speak up, or your head will be chopped in an instant and your limbs maliciously torn apart one by one. Let's see this company of wolves, for the vermin that they are.

Naturally, corporate cultures have rapidly degenerated into colonies of boot-camps in which overworked minions dart frantically about behaving like bees in a hive. These spineless conformists are deemed the heroes in this New World Order. Nonetheless, nothing new and creative can ever come from such a rigid and regimented mindset that now composites the swamp of humanity. As **George Bernard Shaw** once said:-

"The reasonable man adapts himself to the world; the unreasonable one persists in trying to adapt the world to himself. Therefore, all progress depends on the unreasonable man."

Nevertheless, blackballing and venomous gossip is still tolerated in many circles. Were one to indulge in the same vile rhetoric publicly, they would be rapidly sued for slander. Similarly, many surf on established hate groups to denigrate an entire race, minority, sect or religion. It seems there is no crime, if one has powerful enough buddies. So collective evil is allowed to proliferate in cases where its very insidiousness should matter the most. It has become a powerful force that keeps us all feeling separate and alienated from one another.

(Jesus) If you are finished with your venting feast, I will now proceed!

Firstly, you must realize that even small problems at the collective level can soon compound to have enormous consequences. For example, the loss of a particular member of a species can soon destroy an entire ecosystem. Likewise, credit card fraud, phishing e-mails, and information wars started in small pockets in distant countries can quickly escalate to exert a hazardous influence on the worldwide economy. The *butterfly effect* has demonstrated admirably, that even our most minor acts or thoughts can be globally felt and often result in endless repercussions. What is evident is the following.

(1) Problems do not exist in isolation. They continuously interchange between the individual and the collective.

(2) Small problems can quickly become immense and pervasive. One person's minor health problem today may be tomorrow's pandemic.

(3) Problems continuously change from one form into another. When a trivial issue or concern is denied or repressed where it needs to be dealt with, it can soon manifest in a whole different direction and form. So one, who is forced to suppress their sexuality or gender identity may develop a severe addiction, while one who feels alienated and unheard may become a suicide bomber, like Timothy McVeigh.

(4) We all collectively own all the world's problems. This may not be very obvious at first, but look closely enough, and you will see that it is so. The macrocosm reflects the microcosm and vice versa. When any individual's problems are left to go unresolved for long, this can result in destructive and hostile behaviors. Since behavior breathes behavior, the chain of hostility can soon pass from one to another.

Similarly, we are all rewarded and healed when anyone's individual problems are corrected. In their healing and return to sanity lies our own. A peaceful and tranquil mind, anywhere, soon becomes a blessing to all. So one who decides to live a simple and bucolic life, never taking more than they need will not be radiating stress and anxiety to others. He or she will not be driving like a nutcase on the highway. By avoiding accidents and deaths, they will be reducing everyone's insurance and medical costs. These folk can thus become the harbingers who exterminate all the toxic BS and meaningless strife out of our society.

Yes, they are the immediate beneficiaries, but their peace, joy, and example soon circulate to all. Each can become the inheritor of their inspiring example. When we all develop a more collective attitude and recognize the enormous impact of our decisions and behaviors, the progress can be asymptotic.

(5) No problem will disappear until it is resolved at its root. This is most critical because a problem will continue to roam until it is healed there.

Often a plethora or seeming unrelated problems can be traced back to a single root. **However, there is one Über problem that is at root of all our problems and that is our belief in separation.** That is the sole cause of all problems one will ever know. All are interconnected and ultimately traceable back to this single root. We have already explored some of the fundamental problems caused by our belief in separation, including the birth of the ego and the development of our split-minds. The decisive impact is that we have become blind to our erroneous patterns of thought and have begun to think of ourselves as mere bodies inhabiting a spacetime existence. This in turn strengthens the world of illusions and provides it with a moderately believable foundation.

Likewise, all who believe fully in separation will take themselves to be bodies and therefore be in fear. Hence they will judge and exploit and build countless unneeded defenses to protect their interests and to guard themselves against other bodies. So arises a world of so many distortions and miscreations of mind. One that denies Truth and hinders one from reaching Knowledge of their real Identity.

Meanwhile the numerous defenses we establish through fear results in increased isolation. It functions as a major impediment to our healing and happiness. As a result, light is barred from entering our awareness. The fearful world that emerges from this belief in separation comes at a great cost. Since the "separated" invest in both sin and guilt, they use these to "justify" all their attacks and to reinforce their illusory partitions with others. All the time denying unity and innocence. Yet it is only through regaining awareness of one's divine innocence and holiness that one can heal.

THE DOG OF THE EGO

There once lived a happy dog. However, this dog grew annoyed with his tail always wagging behind him. So he bit it off. Then, one day his skin started to irritate and itch. As a result he kept nibbling at this until he became a very mangy looking dog. Shortly after this, he felt his legs were too slow. So he chewed at them until they became totally non-functional. Now all was OK, except for those annoying earflaps continuously smacking against his ears. It seemed like a minor inconvenience at first, but it soon escalated, and he took the appropriate action.

Then he noticed that his tongue was perpetually dribbling saliva all over his feet. So he bit down hard until deeply lacerated it fell to the ground. Now he enjoyed a few hours of peace before he became severely depressed with his nose. There it was, always protruding ahead of him, blocking his vision. Hence he broke all his teeth in his frantic efforts to chomp it off. When this failed, he began darting into nearby walls, hoping to knock it out of place. However, all he succeeded in accomplishing was gouging his eyeballs out of their sockets.

The dog remains today, totally emaciated, exhausted and blind. He has gone quite mad from listening to all the ringing in his ears. Nevertheless, he scampers about from place to place powered by broken legs and paws. Unable to lap or eat, he becomes weaker by the day. Now and then, when he can muster up enough energy, he makes another attempt to knock his nose out of place. Yes, it seems the sense of smell is always the last to go.

This dog represents our ego selves. Alienated from our true Identity, we now go trolling madly about in the relative existence. Forever restless, we project our failures and unease always to an external cause. It is always another who is the cause of our loss of peace. Our first instinct, therefore, is to snap at those who distract us. We do recognize them as our tail, who can help demonstrate our friendliness to all. Those who irritate the hell out of us are our skin. Endlessly criticizing our poor decisions, they always rub us the wrong way. Thus we are ungrateful for the protection and buffer they provide. Nevertheless it is they who help us to avoid many greater mistakes. Instead, we want to sink our teeth into them and disown them from our lives. Those flapping unpredictably nearby are our ear-flaps. They help dampen and filter out the tinnitus of our self-absorption and the screeching sounds of our insanity. They enable us to hear without any trace of bias.

Then there are those who pander to our every word, who help disseminate our profound message to the main-stream. Not recognizing these faithful supporters, as our tongue, we dismiss them as plagiarizers and idle gossipers. In consequence, we want to bite down hard and tear them out of our lives. Likewise there are the Holy Ones, who provide the vision and raw understanding that can help us perceive the underlying unity in all. These are teachers of an ancient wisdom and powerfully reflect the innermost part that remains in contact with Truth. They enable us to smell our way out of illusion and to rise far above the dark mantle of the relative world. Unfortunately, we have be-come blind to their gifts. We prefer to spend our days chas-ing idly after idiotic desires and banging into the walls of judgment and prejudice. However, these Holy Ones our egos are forever powerless to bite.

However, the dog of the ego cannot comprehend all this. Perceiving itself as separate, it remains at war with all. It mercilessly deploys its sword of judgment to cut us off from others. Failing to see the landscape of perception as merely a mirror, it has us wander about feeling incessantly tired, hungry and worn down. In its unwillingness to join with the fountain of healing, it keeps us feeling sick, isolated and victimized.

Alas! with a better interpretation of our world, we would quickly discern that those behind us on the path are extending the gifts of patience and clarity. They enable us to clarify our messages until it gains in strength. By ridding us of all false distortionary beliefs, they empower our minds to crystallize with perfect Knowledge. Those next to us on the life journey are kindred spirits who can expeditiously accelerate our learning and growth. From these, we can rapidly learn just as much, as we can teach. Then there are those up ahead, who are the light-bearers, who wonderfully demonstrate our success is guaranteed. Having overcome the ego in themselves, they illustrate the heights of greatness, that are possible.

LEARNING DEVICES

(Sharon) In *"A Course In Miracles,"* you describe our great need of learning devices. You actively teach how they are of enormous benefit for transcending the world and regaining awareness of our divine perfection. **I would be grateful if you could go into more detail and explain how they can be most efficaciously engaged.**

(Jesus) You will use this world either as your hunting grounds or else as your healing oasis. This projected holo-motion picture is designed to continuously test you. It is a divine alchemist that is masterful at eliciting the very worst in you and it forces you to continuously learn and improve. All the same, it can often feel merciless in its ways. Just a few wrong moves, on your part and you can suddenly feel the blade at your throat. Even so, your values and virtues are not real until proven out on the stage of life.

The real question then is how you will respond? Will you become savage or compassionate? Hopelessly depressed or euphoric? Closed-off and rigor-mortis or continuously adventurous and playful? A three-year-old with an incredible curiosity is no great thing, but an eighty-three-year-

old, who has retained an insatiable curiosity is one definitely to be admired.

To continuously endorse the ego is to invite spiritual suicide. You will feel each of your psychological limbs torn off
one by one and those inner eyeballs, needed for vision,
brutishly plucked out of their sockets. Whenever you empower the ego to become Master over your life, know well
that misery, anguish, and despondency are soon on the
way. You will then find out in no uncertain terms, that
there can be far worse things than dying.

Nonetheless, in your mind also lies your sanctuary of healing. It is a place where you can gain in strength and power
and fast become a luminous being in the eyes of others. To
accomplish this, you need to develop trust in something far
greater than your ego self. Something infinitely higher and
wiser. Reach to a pure and noble goal that leaves no one
outside the Holy circle. For the Spirit in you aims to bring
salvation to all. For this, you must become willing to open
your mind and abandon all your ego motivated agendas.
You must fire yourself as your own teacher so as to be re-
born into the bonfire of Truth. You must recognize all unhappiness is caused by yourself. It propagates from your
ignorance, incorrigible attitudes, selfish thoughts and be-

haviors. So long as you remain clinging to a false image in a dream, nursing unsatisfying goals and shallow self-obsessions, you can never arrive at any authentic happiness and growth.

Once you realize your greatest need is to dispossess all wrong-minded beliefs, you begin to pave your way towards perfect understanding. Then all your fears and circumventing thoughts melt away, and you reach unconditional peace.

"Those who remember always that they know nothing, and who have become willing to learn everything, will learn it. But whenever they trust themselves, they will not learn. They have destroyed their motivation for learning, by thinking they already know. Think not you understand anything until you pass the test of perfect peace, for peace and understanding go together and can never be found alone."

[ACIM, T-14.XI.12:1-4]

In the Course, I taught that learning devices are vital to conveying Truth back into your awareness. By removing all stumbling blocks to your vision, they markedly accelerate your progress. Over time they establish an inner platform that boosts your capacity for making faultless evaluations. Employing them wisely, you become greatly invigorated and simultaneously increase in clarity and joy. Unless you harness the power of learning devices, you will remain unaware of your divine perfection and continue to endure severe conflicts within. You will wallow and flail aimlessly in a sea of toxic emotional states. Being fundamentally unstable, you will oscillate from one moment to the next as a community of hypocritical selves that are all imposters to the throne.

Learning devices are the boat that ferries you to the other shore. They can help you to clearly distinguish what constitutes meaningful purpose. Enable you to undergo meaningful, life renewing transformations. The only worthwhile ambition for the mind is restoring its lost connection to Spirit and its Knowledge. All other goals attract with worthless gifts and are transient in nature. They rob you of all energy and leave you depleted in a void of disillusionment. Learning devices, in contrast transport you out of the world of illusion and bring Truth back into your awareness. By undoing all effects of the original error, they restore your mind to its original state of purity, bliss, and radiance. Once you arrive at the other shore, the boat is to be abandoned. The final purpose of all learning devices, being to obviate themselves. Learning devices can be used most strategically to save you from drowning in a sea of illusions. Using them judiciously, you are rafted expeditiously out of the world of darkness.

It is extremely difficult to learn under the wrong conditions. Unless the necessary motivation is established and permanently ingrained, progress will be slow and painful. Each develops this motivation intellectually at first and then viscerally. For a while, this world will fool and bedazzle you and completely bewitch your senses. Only when you fully comprehend that you always walk away empty-handed, will you begin to question its value. Slowly you come to realize this world is nothing but a halfway house and it has no real gifts to bequeath. To see this hopeless, convoluted maze, for what it is, is the decision to leave the human jungle.

Depression, suffering, and despair can be greatest teachers to viscerally motivate you. They can be seen as badges of honor, worn by those who have continuously invested effort where it has failed. In savage states of depression, one begins to peer through all the smoke and mirrors of the ego's thought. To finally discern its sad and depressing curriculum for what it is — a vain and futile journey, that can offer no hope of success! A mindless space odyssey that fools only the very superficial. Some will not reach this point of despair until they arrive at the ninth circle of Dante's hell. Sooner or later everyone is awoken.

"Being faced with an impossible learning situation is the most depressing thing in the world. In fact, it is ultimately why the world itself is depressing."

[ACIM, T-8.VII.8:3-4]

Absolute despair is the great liberator and it presents your most excellent learning opportunity. It is the moment when you become finally ripe for Enlightenment. Despair is an illuminator because it communicates, very expeditiously, the news that all worldly dreams must end in failure. So it entices you to emerge from the frozen cocoon of your denial and to conscientiously open your mind. It inspires you to become more fully present to the present. In an instant, you become cogently aware of a far more sub-

tle, satisfying and potent reality that has always surrounded you. One never noticed before. Now, brimmed with en-
thusiasm, the path becomes clear.

You asked what are these learning devices of the mind! A
learning device is anything the Holy Spirit uses to accelerate your progress towards Truth. However, I will go into
three in detail. Since they are fundamental and of utmost
importance to understand. Namely **(1) Spacetime** and **(2)
Consciousness** and the **(3) The body**.

Spacetime, as you are aware is an unreal artifice that you
have mentally projected. Your spacetime perceptions always reflects the evolutionary progression in your learning. Thus they image in form the composite of your beliefs.
This artifice will disappear when all your beliefs and understandings are 100% harmonious with Truth. This requires an absolute state of congruency in which you retain
nothing that is false.

The purpose of all learning is to subtract away all your
false knowledge so that Truth can be revealed. Your
spacetime journey then is therefore simply one of relinquishment. You unburden yourself of that which never ex-

isted and thus eliminate all miscreations and hallucinations arising from your misplaced beliefs.

Consciousness, on the other hand, is the learning device associated with evolving mental concepts. All ideas you hold reflect both the purity of your understanding and your capacities for mental abstraction. Employing this learning device rightly leads to an inner spiritual evolutionary progression, in which all your concepts become more expansive and light-filled. Eventually, you become capable of going beyond the symbolic and reaching to the supra-conceptual existence of Truth. You apprehend a far more transcendent reality that no concept can ever point towards. At this stage your consciousness and perception become unnecessary and disappear from your mind. Hence you are no longer bound to this very limiting operational mode of experiencing.

In the meantime, you will continue to play games with various symbols, concepts, and forms so as to broaden them and bring them into alignment with timeless Truth. Some of these games include the resolution of various contradictions, dualities, and mental paradoxes. Reason and inward evolution help you gain a far broader perspective. Epiphanies and lifetimes of experience can also be of tremendous help.

The body is an essential learning device. Deployed correctly, you will use it exclusively to communicate Truth. Thus you rapidly dissolve all false notions of separation and become reintegrated and healed. Miracles, Holy Instants, and experiences of Revelations are all powerful learning devices that position one further along in time. The 365 Course lessons, I gave, can be catalytic to your progress.

It is a great mistake to think the function of learning is to know. The real purpose of learning is to discover that you know not. Only then will you freely dispossess yourself of all that is faulty or limiting in your Self-understanding! Once all erroneous patterns of thought have been released, Truth will come naturally of its own. In the meantime, one must learn to live openly and fearlessly in the crisp thin air of uncertainty.

Only those who are open-minded, trusting, playful, present and non-attached can broaden their view and penetrate through to the mysterious, miraculous and intangible dimensions of existence. Doing so your life become a meaningful adventure towards Truth. Along the way, you will be undergoing a beautiful metamorphosis and come into complete awareness of perfect Being. One-by-one, all the barricades of false knowledge will fall away until you arrive at the surety of Knowledge. With each passing day, you will feel lighter in step, having relinquished that weighty, burdensome rucksack of falsities on the hot and dusty road. Your nascent awareness will be suffusing you with waves of endless joy and transforming you into an impressive living dynamo of potent action. For you are reaching now to that holy fountain, which alone can quench all thirst.

Now, as you knock back a cool one, you wonder why you had spent millions of years collecting worthless garbage to decorate the walls of your prison-house. Why had you blinded yourself so pervasively with the dust of ignorance? Yes, you had become like an old decrepit vagabond pushing your supermarket trolley of junk, aimlessly about in the Texas heat. Allowed your mind to become so dull and dead with lusterless information. You had cataloged numerous redundant esoteric facts, that had only confused you further. You had tried to make the worthless valuable. Then you wondered why you were not happy. Your lights were out — that is why!

The purpose of learning is to remove all this junk from the room. That tattered coat, the broken doll, and that shiny hobgoblin over there. All colorful trinkets you had overly esteemed, as if they held the very keys to your salvation. You must question and interrogate all now to assess its eternal value. As you survey your world with new eyes, you sense the air becoming a little less stale. You are no longer suffocating with dread, as if you were being buried alive. There was no air percolating through the window of your soul. Nothing to connect you with spirit and rejuvenate your being.

Finally, the hint of an ancient wisdom is crossing into your mind, energizing to life new springs of hope. You are becoming more expansive and radiant. An expert in distilling content from form. No longer dazzled by complexity of form but looking to content alone. You are preparing your altar to receive timeless wisdom. Now you recognize that all objects, idols, and phenomena that tantalized your senses were just many different faces of one problem — your belief in separation. Yet, what is separation, but an ego dream of self-sufficiency? One in which you mistakenly think you can successfully operate apart from the divine.

You only believed you were separate from Reality because you interposed this alien will before it. This did not invalidate Truth, it just hid you away in a private world. One, in which you felt powerless to heal your distortions. It must be becoming evident now, that most of your beliefs are ill-founded. That they just distort all your perceptions and inhibit the true light of your Being.

Untrue beliefs propel your mind along the dark paths of magic and miscreation. They build a hallucinatory universe and induce your mind deeper into sleep. Ensnared in this private kingdom of specialness, you become truly crazed and roam about the palace like King George. Nevertheless, learning devices are here for your rescue. They will help purge all that is false including:-

1. *Your Belief in an Objective Spacetime Existence.*

2. *Your Belief in Separation.*

3. *Your Belief that you have Power apart from God.*

4. *Your Belief that Idols can complete you and bring lasting Happiness.*

5. *Your Beliefs in Evil, Sin, Sacrifice, Suffering and Death and all other illusory miscreations of the ego.*

6. *Your Belief in an outside power that can hold you Ransom.*

7. *You Belief that the Inner is separate from the Outer. That Cause and Effect are divided and independent.*

8. *All Magical Beliefs.*

9. *Your Beliefs in victimization and of being unfairly treated.*

10. *Your Beliefs that the Body, Consciousness, and Perception are all Absolutes, rather than mere learning devices of the mind, to be best employed for healing.*

11. *Your Belief that Fear is Real and not just the product of thinking with the ego.*

THE TWO FISHERMEN

(Sharon) From where I stand, it seems unlikely that we will ever dislodge our almost irreversible beliefs, in so may things you mention. They have become so deeply embedded in our living experience, that it is hard to see how learning devices will ever be of help.

(Jesus) You only continue to believe such things because you lack faith in the Real. You have no faith, as yet in the power of the Eternal.

(Sharon) Yes, you keep talking in such glowing terms about the power of Miracles, Holy Instants, and Revelations to save us. When are you going to come down into the real world of specifics? I think Helen was correct when she said the "The Course" was far too generalized to be of much help to most.

(Jesus) Faith is not a freebie. It has to be earned in the world of time. You increase your faith, through making right decisions. This part alone is up to you! The divine has no power to overrule you because you are part of the Mind of God. Freedom, Bliss, and unconditional Trust can never be known by those who enable tyranny to reign in the place of True Power.

You need to start off by making baby steps. Thus will you gain the spiritual conviction, that the laws of God alone are true! Your faith can easily move mountains and even raise the dead because there is no order of difficulty to miracles. Let me relate to you a story about two fishermen that may better elucidate this.

A very skilled fisherman came to this deep dark ancient lake. He was hoping to catch enough fish to sustain himself and his family. He fished silently, all day but did not land a single catch. He was a little surprised being confident in his abilities and never having had this problem before. Nevertheless, being very upbeat and dedicated he returned the very next morning at dawn. Once again he cast out his line and waited patiently for his moment of glory. He fished until dusk, trying every conceivable type of bait, but came away empty handed. He was now more determined than ever that this lake would not get the better of him. It was all-out war! Still convinced there must be copious fish in this lake, he came every day at dawn and remained until late into the night. It did not matter whether it rained, hailed or snowed, he remained undeterred. His wife and family were beginning to think he had gone completely nuts and turning into a Captain Ahab.

Over the ensuing months, his self-belief started to wane. By the end of six months, his confidence was conclusively destroyed — hook, line, and sinker. He even began to rationalize his zealous madness by confidently insinuating that the lake had no fish in it after all. At that moment, utterly defeated, he decided to just give up! Walking away from it all, he felt his dignity and self-esteem were irreparably shattered. As he was heading back, wholly dejected, he noticed another fisherman come along and cast his line from the exact same spot; he had used. Within minutes, this fisherman had landed the most gainful fish he had ever seen. So what is the moral of this story?

(Sharon) It sounds like the story of my life. I keep throwing out my line, fishing for fish and other opportunities that never come along. It seems my efforts are wasted, and I never land the big one. **But if I were to hazard a guess, I would say, it was a story about Faith!**

(Jesus) Yes! And which of these fishermen had the most faith?

(Sharon) The first one. He had the belief and commitment to come every day and endure through all extremes of weather and hardship. His faith just never paid off, and he should not be judged harshly for his resilience and fortitude. Had he less faith and more common sense, he might have given up within the hour. Gone to another lake, that paid higher dividends. It seems his faith worked against him! The second fisherman just got lucky. Now he must be all pumped up and have great faith and confidence in his fishing capacities. Nevertheless, his faith is all just an illusion born out of pure luck.

(Jesus) There is no such thing as luck. Nothing ever comes at random! If luck were real, God's justice would be a sham! Yes, there is much, that seems like luck, but be not deceived and do not become embittered by the spontaneous success of others. Grace is a Heavenly reward extended to those who have earned it painfully over lifetimes. By eradicating negative beliefs and redirecting misplaced faith, they have come into spiritual harmony and thus deserve all the grace that freely flows their way. The ego, not understanding this, substitutes spontaneous God-given grace with its concept of luck. It then uses "Luck" to nourish bitterness and dissent. Engaging it destructively against your own best interests. When life is just marvelous and peachy, and things are falling effortlessly into place, the ego uses your good fortune to empower itself in your mind and thought. It endlessly preaches how this for-tuitous stream of events is the natural outcome of follow-ing its advice.

Then when luck turns against you and the world becomes savage, it employs your misfortune, as further evidence that the world is your enemy. Its advice is that you protect your private interests at all costs, even it means becoming overtly brutal, merciless, selfish and self-absorbed. Now remember these words I spoke in the Course.

"Now you must learn that only infinite patience produces immediate effects. This is the way time is exchanged for eternity. Infinite patience calls upon infinite love, any by producing results *now* it renders time unnecessary."

[ACIM, T-5.VI.12:1-3]

The second fisherman had great faith built up over past lifetimes of pain, effort, and failure. But his faith was not in himself. It was unshakeable trust in the power of God, to set all things right. Of himself, he knew he was nothing and could accomplish nothing.

The first fisherman, on the other hand, was still very worldly and calculating. He had no essential trust in existence and was constantly on guard against uncertainties to come. His only belief was in his personal abilities and strength. In other words, he only believed in his ego self. Anyone who places their trust exclusively in the ego must eventually be humiliated and shamed. The second fisherman had been like this once too and had to painfully eviscerate the myth of his personal power through millennia of failures. He had to be stripped bare of all the foolishness which the world bestowed so that he could fully recognize the unfailing, limitless and eternal power of the divine within.

MASTERY AND PERFECTION

(Sharon) I must tell you now a story about my friend Dr. Gobbler's Knob and then solicit your input.

I hadn't seen him in the longest while. He had just returned from a trip to Argentina. While there, he had developed a passion for quaffing back the most aged cognacs and smoking fine cigars. He was all excited about his trip, telling me about his adventures to both Iguazu falls and the small seaport town of Ushuaia, all on the same day. Apparently, it was snowing hard in Ushuaia when he arrived, even though he had been sweltering in the jungle earlier that day. Then he went on a boat excursion to the lighthouse at the end of the world, which Jules Verne had written about in one of his novels.

EVITA'S FINAL RESTING PLACE

In any case, when the venerable Dr. finally got back to Buenos Aires, he started getting wasted early in the day and began hanging out in the Recoleta district. He visited Evita's grave, which he held sacred. Then he wandered about the graveyard for a while. All the stone porticoes, marble mausoleums and wilted flowers somehow enchanted him. Since he did not give a toss about the other deceased dignitaries he started chasing stray cats idly about. Then fascinated to know exactly what they got up, he climbed in after one, to one of the Marble mausoleums. There tired and drunk, he soon fell asleep. When he woke up, it was already dark, and there was this foul and wicked stench everywhere. He was nauseous and spooked and felt outnumbered by the army of the dead. He had to get out of there fast. Besides he was almost sober now and his drinking hours were numbered.

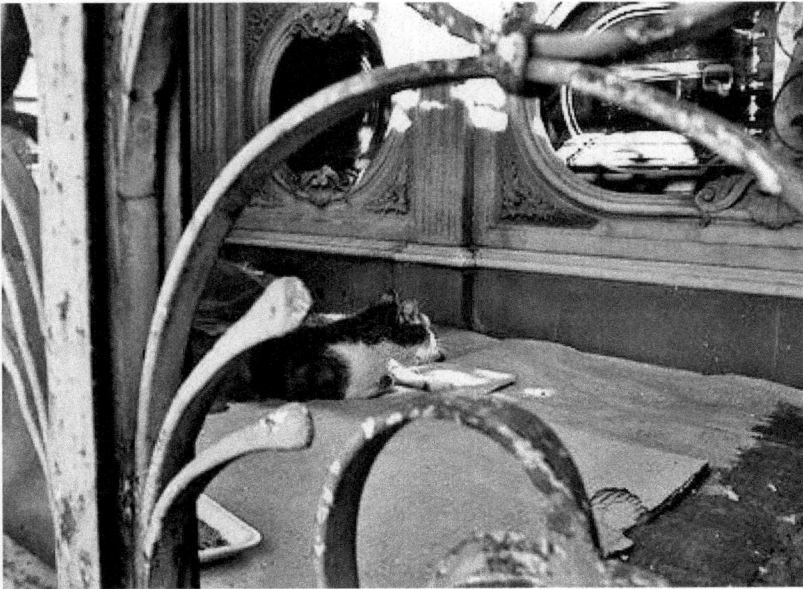

ONE OF THE CAT'S IN THE GRAVEYARD

Immediately he headed to La Boca and took in a Tango show. Soon he was spifflicated all over again. All he needed now was some erotica, so he took a taxi to the gay bars in Barrio Norte. There with his few words of Spanish he managed to snare some nice new friends. He was glad to be rubbing shoulders with these denizens from down below. The pussy whipped part of the world, as he saw it. He even entertained some hookers by reading their palms and so he dished it out to impress them. *"Su línea de vida es muy larga pero su corazón está roto."* Before long this turned out to be a real icebreaker and he had the hookers hooked.

He soon found himself high up in the hills, at a party and the very center of attention. He was beginning to have those delusions of grandeur, thinking himself completely sui generis with his dark shades and whiskey bottle dangling out from his jacket pocket. Of course, there was also his peace pipe carefully hidden way in his socks. All the same, he was not quite sure how he had gotten there and surmised he must have blacked out somewhere along the way. Then, as he reached back into his pocket, he noticed his wallet was gone. He could not believe it. He had always used his money belt as a decoy. Now he realized, he had even forgotten the name of his hotel. So where was he to direct a taxi to? He was — Fucked! Fucked! Fucked! and at the complete mercy of all these strangers.

As he was recounting this tale of his travels, he suddenly switched gears and changed topics. So he asked in a very muted, sincere and direct voice *"Sharon, Are you a Master?"* I was taken aback by the sudden change of direction. He had never asked anything remotely like this before. It is one of those questions that will damn you, either way you respond. Then he said, *"Stop pussyfooting around and swashbuckling me. Give me a simple* **Yes** *or* **No.** *There is no such thing as being half a Master.*"

So I ask, "What is the best way to respond to the Dr.'s question?"

(Jesus) You are on the ball; it is a dangerous question to answer. If you had answered "**Yes**," he would come to hate you in the long-term because no ego can ever tolerate feeling less, than anyone else. Most certainly, he would have exacted some form of vengeance or ridiculed you when the opportunity best presented itself, This is why most Masters shut their mouths and keep quiet. Look at the faith that met all those Masters, like myself, who had proudly self-declared our Self-Realization. As you can recall, I was denied, abandoned, beaten, lashed and humiliated. The twisted egos of most could not stand to feel inferior, even for any instant. So they used every measure possible to pull me down, ridicule and humble me.

Never underestimate the ego's powers of imagination, craftiness, and ingenuity when it comes to inflicting maximal pain and humiliation. That crown of thorns and vinegar in my wounds really did prepare me for that red carpet event up Mount Calvary. But don't you worry because everyone gets crucified sooner or later by the world. My friends Al Hallaj. Socrates and Osho all met similar fates, as did Joan of Arc. Al Hallaj was torn apart limb from limb, Socrates was poisoned, Joan of Arc was burned at the stake and Osho was merely hounded and blackballed out of existence. Refused entry to twenty-three countries. Other Self-Realized beings like Krishnamurti, the Buddha, Meher Baba, Ramakrishna, Sri Aurobindo and Vivekananda were endlessly pursued by followers, who would not stop pestering them.

Even Sri Ramana Maharshi was not let off the hook. Once he was discovered, he got very little free time to meditate in his cave. He was unfailingly stalked by those spiritual hippies coming in by the container-load from the western world. All they wanted to do was to talk, talk, talk and have him present some sermon. Some words to temporarily sedate from all their ego miseries and deficiencies.

Only a rare few avoided the trap. Milarepa, Bodhidharma, Lao Tzu and the Wanderling are some prime examples. They pulled their hats down over their eyes, metaphorically speaking of course. Milarepa, unfortunately, turned green from eating all that repulsive nettle soup. Bodhidharma stripped his eyelids off and threw them to the ground. This worked wonderfully to put the fear of God in any who dared ask any questions. If they asked him for illumination, he would arbitrarily demand they bring him their minds the very next morning on a plate, which really set them tripping. Only Huike was up to the challenge. Only he was fearless and pure enough to cut off his arm and throw it down before Bodhidharma. Thus he received the gift that always gives.

Meanwhile, Lao Tzu headed into the desert of Mongolia where no one wanted to go. Yes, these few kept themselves below the radar, so as not to become a feeding ground for the flies. Anyway, how did you respond to the Dr.?

(Sharon) I crisply responded, "*If you don't know by now, I am not going to tell you. Because such a question cannot be answered by mere words. It must be felt deep in your being and bone. Sensed by your intuition and innermost eyes of Spirit. No words from me are ever going to make a hoot of a difference. It is only your ego that wants answers at the level of words. It is always circling about, nourishing itself on the superficial because it cannot know anything directly. It only feels comfortable and safe when everything is nicely labeled and put away in its box. This furnishes it with the illusions of knowledge and control. Nonetheless, it is incapable of enter-*

ing the mysterious dimensions, for such knowledge would burn and destroy it."

(Jesus) Nice One! I couldn't have answered it better! So what happened then?

(Sharon) He was taken aback and behaved like I was just maneuvering to swindle him or buy more time. Nevertheless, I could see his deep distress, which promptly manifested as excruciating nervousness and twitchiness. All of a sudden his legs and arms went fluttering about in all directions and were no longer under his conscious control. Then he started scrambling to land a low blow, so as not to be outshone. He quickly vociferated, *"At least, Skywalker, is a Master. That, I know, for sure!"*

To which, I responded, *"You mean Skywalker, the cutter, whose arms are so lacerated and crosshatched with the signature of his own blade that they even put the notches on the tree next to the Donner party to shame? The guy who has made cutting into some new form of street art, akin to engraving a Pablo Picasso painting into one's body. One who supervises his own Masterpieces through demonized, craze-filled eyes."*

All the same, I had to admit Skywalker certainly had his well-earned stripes. He was like a leopard, forever on the prowl and ready to go in for the kill. Except his Serengeti was that sickly, sweat infused lustful arena of thundering flesh, found only in the modern city.

Then the Dr. responded, "*Skywalker definitely is a Master of sorts, he is a Master in the field of life.*"

This, I also had to concede. Skywalker had never begged for a penny in his life, even after spending three years homeless. He even turned in a wallet, loaded with cash to the local police, when he could no longer afford a coffee. Yes, Skywalker was most definitely that one in a thousand, or two in ten thousand, you have spoken off before. One whose values are serenely unshakeable and whose integrity always gleams in brilliance. One who moves unimpeded through life with the effortless grace and color of a butterfly and the fierceness of a lurking tiger.

THE BODILY IDENTITY

(Jesus) Most diagnose very external causes to their pain. They get obsessed with what is appearing on the periphery and are unwilling to explore any deeper.

They are continuously bombarded with feelings of anxiety, sadness, fear, apathy and rage. The usual suspects, so to speak. Even so, when asked to pinpoint the real source of their discontent, they are likely to be way off target. That is they will automatically project all the blame to superficial causes, such as their financial problems, job, family issues or relationships. Alternatively, they may see the torment-ing cause in a rigged economy, unfair social system, an un-caring world or the instability and pollution of their im-mediate environment. Then there are all their addictions, out-of-control spending habits, personality distortions, self-image issues and of course the neighbor's crying baby. Most feeling the deck stacked against them never discern the body as at the root of all their problems.

However, without a body, no one could ever experience this bleak landscape of separation and would be cured of all ills. When we probe a little deeper, we see that the body's relentless stream of demands absorbs most of our energy and time. It is forever presenting us with an avalanche of needs, including those for food, shelter, protection, healthcare, exercise and rest. Likewise, it usually insists on having some form of transport, to ferry it about in style from one meaningless vortex point in the dream to another. Since money is always needed to support it, one feels forced into mental prostitution to the corporations, bartering their brain for bucks. So spending the best part of their lives working a deluge of mindless jobs.

Let's not forget that endless plethora of communication devices needed to create its online image, which in turn provide it with the illusion that it is friends with other bodies. Being so vulnerable and easily prone to sickness, one soon becomes subsumed by its vital need for innumerable medications, healing remedies, inoculations, health screenings, therapies, and cures. Add to this the vast expenditures of time and effort spent beautifying the body. All those mandatory facials, perms, manicures and full-body massages. Some may even require a pygmy stepping on their back, executing some primal dance, to remove some tension in their lower lumbar.

The ego is insufferable in its coercion and always wants you to fashion your body into some very trendy and prominent specimen of beauty, agility and strength. This starts out, harmlessly enough, with various gym and yoga club memberships, followed by wearing some glorifying rags in public. All aimed at propagating the myth of your celebrity, exclusivity, and eminence to others. But soon you feel compelled to undertake a vast litany of plastic surgeries including liposuctions, nip-tucks, collagen injections, blepharoplasties, rhinoplasties, abdominoplasties and so on ad infinitum.

It is sad to see so many, spending most of their resources making repairs to a burning house. However, they see this burning house as their temple of salvation. Disappointed, they project their fury squarely upon the body. Somehow, it will just never satisfy them, as their identity and their bitterness, only increases as the years fly down the gutter.

Hence arises the concept of an afterlife which aims to sell each deluded being on some enhanced experience in a hidden paradise. Soon a motley crew of false prophets emerge to capitalize. They emphatically proclaim that no fundamental inner change is needed at all, to get accepted into the inner sanctum sanctorum. Just reel off some prayers and mantras now and then, and light some candles at the Sunday service. However, before you go, give us your women, cash, and undying loyalty. As you can see, any form of organized religion soon degenerates into various forms of religious extremism, genocides, persecutions, pogroms, decapitations and Holy wars.

It must be evident that the body places severe limits on one's natural capacities to communicate. It seems to constrain one to some tiny morsel of the spacetime continuum. So each gesticulates in panic, lest the salt-shaker run out prematurely. Each fervently exploits all forms of communication, at their disposal to get noticed a fraction of a nanosecond longer. This includes engaging in various obscene modes of speech, body language and intimidation while e-blasting viral videos of their inner demons via the hyper-modern conduits of technology. Yes, they must satisfy all their ego's cravings for specialness and pleasure and expunge all weirdness out of their system, before it is too late.

In the process, they transform into assorted oddities, freakazoids and chimerical monstrosities who then troll about spouting gibberish in certain cyber-spaces. Unfortunately, this is not enough. Thus they take extreme pains to cultivate and project their social image even further, often doing so, by painting, cutting or lacerating various exhibitions of color, slash, and gash into their flesh. Yes, every dog must have their stripes, whether it be through the blade, the plastic surgeon or the tattoo artist. Somehow the body cannot be made into a pinnacle of glory and so their pain goes unmitigated. There are many who feel repulsed by it and in their intense dissatisfaction harness every artful or chemical means to compensate for its deficiencies. Thus arises all those pleasure-seeking pursuits, S & M clubs, addictions and prescription drug dependencies.

An organic and human identity is not enough and eventually gives rise to feelings of fear, vulnerability and mortal dread of imminent failure. As the dream progresses, each begins to buy-in completely to various collective forms of fear such as pandemics, epidemics, global warming, space-aliens and international conspiracy theories.

Even so, you may never discern these inner volcanoes, based on the outward projections of bourgeoisie normalcy. For the ego will not allow any bodily self-image to crack, even while undergoing acute emotional, psychological and spiritual meltdowns. Instead, the ego pressurizes all, to sign on the dotted line. The nebulous becomes the norm and concerns you wouldn't otherwise, give a flying f. about now become a matter for holy worship. For once you have accepted the state of separation as real, your spiraling descent is all-but guaranteed. The magical line in the sand, having being drawn-up at the body, establish it as your personal demilitarized zone, that no mortal fiend or succubus shall ever dare pass without facing retaliatory consequences. So emerges a stunning new portrait, that can be so very calculating and vile.

Meanwhile, increasingly groomed and counseled by the ego, you attempt to squash your consciousness in this rotting fetid enclosure. What else are you to do? The body owns you now, hook, line, and sinker.

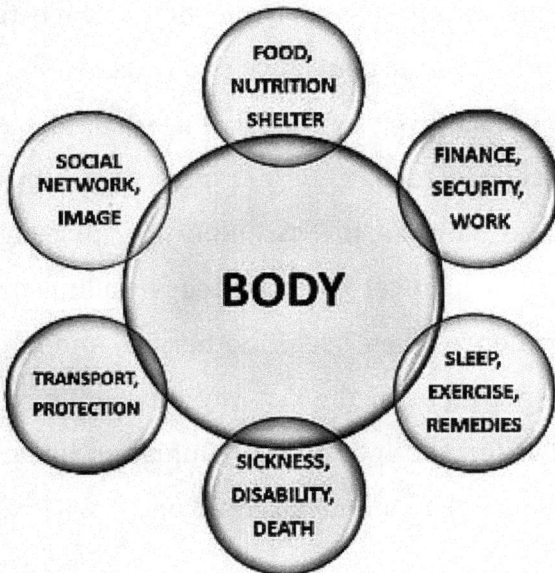

SOME PROBLEMS AND NEEDS ARISING FROM HAVING A BODILY IDENTITY

Once the body has become a firmly conditioned belief, an important inner shift occurs. You no longer relate to it, as just a product of your consciousness. Instead, you see consciousness, as held captive within the body. You begin to think of this pitiful pile of dust as intelligent in its own right. Now, having raised it to Godhood, fear soon proliferates and is given license to kill. Yes, it is only natural, that after apotheosizing the body, thoughts of war, natural disasters, mass starvation and loss creep in and rise to prominence. Simultaneously your mind becomes totally perplexed and confounded by its sad diminutive role in the new scheme of things.

Poisoned by complicity to your bodily investment, all lightheartedness and neutrality soon disappear. You lose as well, the distancing perspective needed, to see it all as dream fiction. Instead, it is seen now as arbitrator of all pleasure and pain. So the assembly line of drugs, addictions, and biochemical escapes keeps rolling in. Soon it gains precedence, even over God herself, and is given the full royal treatment in the runway of your mind. God, in turn, is transformed into a cruel, unjust and heartless demonic monster with a twisted mind and a wicked sense of humor.

Now, you may be beginning to glimpse just part of the cost of holding tight to an unreal identity. All the same, is this identity cast in stone or is it a mere deception? Is the body the real source of all your problems or do they go far deeper? It unmistakably seems to be the root of all problems perceived at the objective level. But are our problems really physical in nature? Or is the body just a patsy we have projected all our deeper problems into?

As I have taught in the Course, the body has never been. Its seeming appearance is entirely due to memory and anticipation. What you must realize, is most of your memories and expectations are driven by distortionary beliefs. Whenever you perceive a body, you are not employing vision but instantiating wish fulfillment in its place. Merely hallucinating then an ego wish into manifestation. For the ego always attempts to have reality on its own pet terms and conditions. It forces all to adapt around its own whimsical needs and preferences.

Nonetheless, wishes can just as easily reflect fanciful desires and strange notions, as anything real. The body represents such a wish, and it can never be made into a reality. Ultimately its appearance arises from impurities in your own Self-understanding. You wish for it, and so it seems to be. Then the ego jumps up in excitement because you have interposed this unworthy barrier between you and your brother. A barrier that keeps your illusions of specialness in place while temporarily assuaging the wrath of God. However, as I said before:

"The body is outside you, and but seems to surround you, shutting you off from others and keeping you apart from them, and them from you. It is not there. There is no barrier between God and His Son, nor can His Son be separated from Himself except in illusions. This is not his reality, though he believes it is."

[ACIM, T-18.VI.9:1-4]

THE BODY AS A LEARNING DEVICE

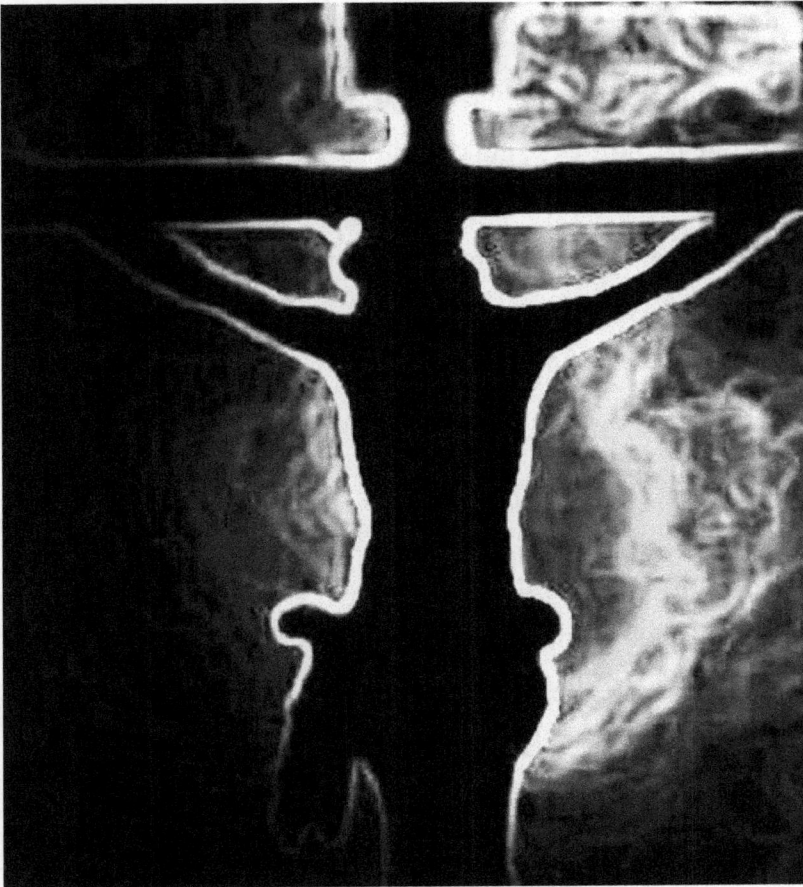

(Sharon) I am beginning to see now how the ego uses the body as a key defense against Truth. However, you also mentioned its possible use as a learning device. **Can you explain how it can be so polarizing in its purpose?**

(Jesus) The body, being nothing but an illusion is power-less in itself. Being illusory, it is entirely neutral and there-fore has no innate or inbuilt capacities. Its health and strength reflect your own beliefs in it and all its modes of sensation are mentally derived. It is the purpose to which you put it then that makes all the difference. You can en-gage it as a very useful tool, to escape the relative existence or else as an impediment, to mire your mind deeper in the mud of the world.

If you retain certain impure wishes for the body, you must also own all their associations. This is the cost of holding onto any false belief and never letting go. You cannot just open a portal to some dark world to grab out something that you like. Some rare trinket, for example, that you feel may emblazon the frame of your specialness. You may not care for anything else down there, but all that is linked must come your way.

Just like in marriage, you cannot simply take the jewel you prize. You will also be inviting in that annoying mother-in-law, the delinquent brother, family debt issues and all their mental sicknesses. Likewise, when you establish bodily temptations or specialness as your wish, you will be ac-cepting all that comes in the fine-print. In will creep all those crippling beliefs in magic, materialism, objectivism, comfort, sickness, suffering, vulnerability, loss and death.

Such bodily desires make the defiant statement that happiness and pleasure are to be found, on the outside. They teach that you are incomplete, as you stand. They, therefore, declare that this landscape of separation is the truth. In summary, this is the belief that *"Ideas can leave their Source within and move around in the form of fast cars, whiskey bottles, blow, easy women and a paradise of such delights."* You may find this belief attractive and think it represents your ticket to independence from other minds. One that licenses you to follow all your unnatural tastes and desires and to go your own evil way. Nonetheless, the serpent, lurking in this Apple, is that you have just made yourself a victim of the world "without."

The Course is not some idea smorgasbord or potpourri of inessentials. You cannot just *pick 'n' mix* those ideas that you like while rejecting those unpalatable to your taste. No! you must imbibe it whole or reject it whole, or else you moor yourself indefinitely on the landscape of contradictory thought and conflicting behavior. This is because all its ideas are perfectly consistent and share the same immutable content. All represent symbolic transmutations of

Truth, specially adapted for the limiting plane of worldly thought.

As we will discuss later, when you dig deep enough into any one of its ideas, you will arrive at all the rest. As with Indra's net, see any of its ideas as impure, unconvincing or lackluster, and you immediately limit the potency of the entire ideational chain of design. Any dark spot will instantaneously become reflected in all the other jewels. When you interpret any of the Course ideas poorly, by seeing them as undesirable or false, you compromise your capacity to receive the gifts the others extend. In contrast, when you appreciate the value in any one and apply its healing power boundlessly, you come to see the same light, potency, and charm, reflected in all.

The ideas presented by the ego can be seductive, alluring and consistent. They can even be easier to grasp at the most superficial levels of your mind. That is from the limited perspective of a separated body, making its way in the world. One must, however, evaluate all ideas in a belief system, based on the results they bring and not just by their decorative wrapping. Under closer examination and application, you discern that the ego's ideas and its belief system fail miserably. Sure, they may temporarily bring some desired results, but these results do not last and cost you so much more. The possibilities of attaining any long-term happiness and peace are myths to the ego, as is any notion of unfolding any increased lovingness within. Nor will you feel any spontaneous outpouring of unity and compassion under its rule. Instead, you will feel only increasing pain, fear, hopelessness, frustration, and a sense of isolation and desperation as the years pass by.

The ego, like all great propaganda machines, sells you on empty ideologies that are poisonous at their core. You start off idealistic and all pumped-up. Soon it sends you to pursue tangential goals. Goals that are either meaningless, insane and unachievable or else represent quick-fix solutions. The longer one pursues them, the more disenchanted and despairing one becomes. Soon you lose all clarity and are in deep confusion. Feeling your mind tearing apart inside, you do not know which way to turn. Like having one foot on the accelerator and the other on the brakes. This may manifest in extreme forms of self-destruction and self-sabotaging behaviors. Ultimately it leads to the ego's most holy aspiration of death.

The ego's belief system functions like all flawed logic. It can be consistent and elegant. However since its fundamental premises stand incorrect, it can never make a single statement or assertion that is veracious. Just a single error and all is rendered junk. Logic does not have the power to determine the inherent falseness or veracity of its premises from within itself. Likewise, the ego is blind to the deceit of its own fallacious beliefs.

For instance, the ego would have you believe, that the body is your salvation, rather than merely a means to your salvation. It sees salvation in its self-made gods of specialness, pleasure, power and adoration. Nonetheless, all who zealously pursue such goals end up disenchanted, isolated, sick and depressed. Specialness, for example, operates by seeking evidence of deep unworthiness in others. That is how it maintains the illusion of its superiority. Thus it ends up friendless. By emphasizing always the unworthiness of others, it comes to see this also in itself.

Any purpose that proclaims the body is an end in itself must lead you to a conflicted position because Spirit could never tolerate such loss. All bodily pleasures being fleeting must exact an equal amount of pain. If you are to fast track your progress, you must shine the inner light on the body and expose all its deficiencies, vulnerabilities and ultimately its unreality. Then you will worship this sacred cow, no longer. Because once, you drop all your investments in it, these ego obstructions and impediments can no longer function as a barrier to vision. Then, in a Holy vision, you will be clearly shown that the body has never been. This mystical experience will fast release you from all meaningless fears and doubts, and all thoughts of death. For then, you will have glimpsed the immaculate picture of something far more transcendent, and well beyond words!

"There is one thing that you have never done; you have not utterly forgotten the body. It has perhaps faded at times from your sight, but it has not yet completely disappeared. You are not asked to let this happen for more than an instant, yet it is in this instant that the miracle of Atonement happens. Afterwards you will see the body again, but never quite the same. And every instant that you spend without awareness of it gives you a different view of it when you return."

[ACIM, T-18.VII.2:1-5]

Reality can only be reached by taking an entirely different approach. One, in which you begin to see the body, as an effect, rather than as a cause. Then, something miraculous begins to happen. Correctly placing the domain of your problems back at their Source can redeem a situation that seems hopeless and infuse it with new life and hope. This powerful epiphany helps you solve your problems at their roots.

DR. GOBBLER'S KNOB STUMBLES INTO DISILLUSIONMENT

It was snowing heavily outside and Dr. Gobbler's Knob was stumbling back from the local pub. He was looking forward to his nice comfortable hotel room. He could not decide what he would do first, relax in the sauna, smoke a Cuban cigar, try one of his marijuana cookies or just knock back some cognacs. While walking back along the streets, he came across a homeless man with no shoes to wear. The man's feet and toes had already gone purplish-blue from the bone-chilling cold. So he dropped a few quarters into his cup, hoping to assuage his guilt. Just then, he heard the man say, *"Bless you kind Sir! I am feeling very privileged tonight because even though I have no shoes, I have met the man who has no feet."*

The Dr. felt an instant stab of compassion. He was experiencing inner volcanoes of emotion that were so rare and alien to him. So off he went to a nearby store and brought back some fine new shoes. Wandering back to his hotel room, he felt happy with himself. Resting up in bed, he had a few nightcaps and began reflecting on his day. He was

proud that he had correctly identified a problem and resolved it.

Next morning it was still snowing heavily outside, as he
headed out for breakfast. Meandering along the streets, he
came across the selfsame bum, from the night before.
There he was happily nursing a 1.75-liter of vodka, show-
ering blessings on all who passed by. The Dr. was instantly
disheartened because the homeless man was no longer
wearing the shoes, he had bought. When he inquired further, the man confessed that they were sold to purchase
the vodka.

Suddenly the Dr. became furious and embittered. He had
been ripped off and cheated by this contemptuous beast
who had exploited him on his act of kindness. He was not
going to be had. So he whipped up the bottle of vodka and
darted off down the street like a leopard on the Serengeti.
He was about to toss it into a nearby bin when he saw a
street prostitute coming his way, after a hard night. She
looked such a wreck that he felt she could do with a pick-
me-up. So he crumbled up one of his marijuana cookies
and poured it into the bottle. Then nonchalantly handed it
out to her, saying *"Here have a shot."* She immediately
glared at him with a ten thousand mile death piercing stare

and said: *"When are you ever going to get real?"* At last, he had found his peace.

PURSUING OUR TROUBLES TO THEIR ROOTS

(Jesus) As you can see when one fails to resolve a problem at its roots, it only seems to go away. **So I ask, what is the real source of this man's problems?**

(Sharon) It seems addiction induced his homelessness, but maybe there is a deeper psychological problem, that he feels powerless to deal with.

(Jesus) The fact that he denies, rather than deals with his problems, is his deeper psychological problem. You see victims abound everywhere on psycho-planet. All desire to jump aboard the victim bandwagon as soon as possible. They want to blame the entire mess of their screwed up lives on some external event or situation. They always bring-up some sad tale from their past that they then dish-out with relish. That fatal event which caused all their addictions, chronic states of homelessness and out-of-control behaviors.

As you tune-in to their rants, you will hear all about their early childhood traumas and tragedies, their unfortunate upbringing and unloving parent(s). The depressed socio-political climate and an uncanny string of bad luck. However, the underlying reality is these "victims" have no real problems at all apart from failing to take any personal responsibility. You will never hear them say this because it strikes too close to the bone! It is much easier to kick the can further down the street and place the blame squarely elsewhere.

(Sharon) Yes, I am cogently aware of all those social parasites and all their slick-willy maneuverings. It seems they will avail of every form of physical, psychological and emotional blackmail on offer, to get what they want. You will never hear them talk about implementing any system of discipline or personal management into their lives because they find it far easier to pass their problems on. After all, why take care of a problem, when you can hijack some other clown or poor bastard to solve it for you? Didn't General Patton say words to such effect?

"I want you to remember that no bastard ever won

a war by dying for his country. He won it by making

the other poor, dumb bastard die for his country."

[*General George Patton*]

Sometimes, it is as straightforward, as our homeless drunk being physically and mentally lazy and preferring drinking to work. That would be the immediate answer, that *Occam's Razor* would provide.

(Jesus) Perhaps! Or he may perceive the world as a fundamentally empty, dissatisfying place and does not want to invest in its ways anymore! Maybe he just escaped from one of those brain-farms that speckle our marvelous landscape and wants no more of the mind-suck and human ownership. Alternatively, he may have a genuine personality disorder that makes it impossible for him to adjust to the stifling soul-crushing routines and pressures?

(Sharon) In any case, I am beginning to see that the original dilemma, of having no shoes on a snowy night can grow increasingly thorny and nebulous, the deeper we probe at its roots. It seems Heisenberg's uncertainty principle kicks in, once we scratch below the surface. The core issue may be entirely variant from one homeless drunk to the next. It seems that for any given set of symptoms there may be multiple possible causes. Only when one success-fully identifies the roots, can they begin to resolve it. Oth-erwise it will just manifest in an alternate form like the many-headed Hydra.

(Jesus) Yes, but most prefer to rationalize their lack of empathy and compassion by arbitrarily assigning causes that are more mentally soothing. They employ all sorts of euphemisms to buffer themselves from all tragic events and injustices in the world around them. For instance, a mean person may pass callously by singing to himself, *"Another homeless drunk too lazy to work."* Thus he ration-alizes his meanness so that it cannot assault his illusory sense of integrity.

The truth is that all the problems you perceive reach far deeper than the body and the world. These are just symp-toms of a far greater problem; we dare never look at. In the ego's scheme, the body is just a patsy opportunistically ex-ploited to divert the focus away from the foundational is-sues. Unfortunately, denial is so powerful that our real is-sues are screened from our conscious awareness. They do not lend themselves therefore to direct frontal assault.

(Sharon) In that case, how should we deal with them?

(Jesus) One can only exterminate all weeds and cobwebs, that grow and flourish in the dark, by letting in the light. The spreading of kindness, blessing, love and inclusion can heal all symptoms arising from fear, meaninglessness, and isolation. When one is in a perpetual state of happiness and contentment and living a purposeful life, all that is nefarious finds it difficult to grow. This calm, quiescent and equanimous state of mind then becomes a natural herbicide that blocks the weeds of rage, frustration, and addiction from appearing and taking root. Because, the latter, are just effects that emerge from an underlying state of unhappiness.

That is why any religious zealots who attempt to sell the concept of eternal life, on its own merits, do not attract many followers. Most are tremendously unhappy in the present and are therefore mortally terrified by the prospect of eternal life! The very thought unleashes wild imaginings of how much more miserable they will be. Delirium and panic sets in because their fundamental dilemma is whether they can just make it to dinnertime, without stringing themselves up.

(Sharon) Yes, it is becoming abundantly clear now, that present happiness, is all we ever seek. If we could just retain that indefinitely, then eternal life would become infinitely more attractive. I think this is why most shudder, whenever they hear the very words **Eternity** or **Immortality**.

Immediately they start conjuring up images of Count Dracula and exsanguination, or of camping out in colonies of vampires, eating rodents for breakfast, dinner, and tea. Or else they freeze up entirely like they are going to be dropped down a dark well, any moment. One from which they will have no chance of escape. The last thing they can conceive of is of some enduring blissful state because this world is not a good preemptive foretaste of any Utopian paradise to come. It seems reaching a state of perpetual happiness, wholeness, and unconditional love is impossible in this relative world.

(Jesus) This is because the bulk of your happiness derives from your many fixations on the external world. Since its gifts are always transitory, fleeting and unstable, so is your happiness. All your ego's means of attaining to happiness do not work. They are bandaids, at best, to temporarily alleviate misery. However, in the long run they induce an equal amount of pain. A state of perpetual happiness can only be reached by uncovering that which is bliss-filled, immaculate and changeless within. Access to your True Being alone can bestow unconditional joy.

Then you become ecstatic with life and find joy in simple things like looking at the moon and stars or listening to the ocean waves. You discover the joy of sharing and of considering others. The joy of making right decisions that have inspiring consequences. When you learn to give without regret, you will seek no longer to take. In contrast, the more complicated your pleasures are, the further you are from true happiness. Then the ego has you hooked.

The body is not going to produce this happiness because the body is far too high-maintenance. Placed beside the immortal treasures that are yours, it is fundamentally worthless. No body can ever be made happy and whole. No body can be loving in itself, and none has any long-term purpose. You, therefore, render yourself unhappy, to the extent that you identify with this sack of blood and bones. Nevertheless, it has come to represent the fundamental fault-line that rivets across all your worlds. Even so, it is only the idle purposes you invest it with that maintain the myth of its existence. Its very appearance makes one feel trashy, worthless, barren and insignificant. You wonder how your immortal spirit and divinity could be locked away inside such a toxic mephitic landfill. This empty frame can hardly be the Masterpiece that God intended. At least it now stands exposed, for what it is. As I said in the Course:-

"Who hangs an empty frame upon a wall and stands before it, deep in reverence, as if a masterpiece were there to see? Yet if you see your brother as a body, it is but this you do."

[ACIM, T-25.II.5:1-2]

So long as you hang all your problems on this clothesline, you can never solve them! Because they are not there but lie far deeper. The body represents just a band-aid thrown into the wind, a flee dancing on the back of a Tyrannosaurus Rex. If you could know this for sure, you would waste no more time on it. I am not asking you to accept, the body as unreal. I am actively imploring you to prove this to yourself. However, I will provide the recipe for doing so. This is not accomplished by jumping out of airplanes or running across beds of nails. Likewise putting it through the racks of pleasure and pain are powerless to discount it. Only by withdrawing all investments in it, will this illusion be exposed.

Even so, each invests wherever they see value. When you see salvation in your mind instead, you will easily pass all limits and penalties the body seems to impose. Then you will reach effortlessly to all and bypass this illusory partition. Spiritual vision, will provide direct experience of having no body! Then you will know the within and without have always been one.

Investing exclusively in your mind, you will one day experience the world implode within. Enter the sea of formlessness and light and reach the forever Real. Know that exquisite and faultless Being that time is powerless to diminish. Realize yourself as that deathless awareness of infinite potency. So do you come to the place of peace, in the quiet eye of the storm! From that moment on, you will no longer mistake illusions for Truth.

(Sharon) Will that vision be permanent or just momentary?

(Jesus) It will be momentary at first and then become more abiding. Nonetheless, even a moment of vision brings great blessings and has tremendous consequences. In that single instant, so many of your current beliefs will go up in smoke. For once, you have seen the body disappear, you will know with certitude that it has always been an image arising from within — that you are the artificer of all worlds you see.

(Sharon) Why do so few gain access to this Vision?

(Jesus) They are fearful of going beyond a certain point in their questioning. They freeze once they are out of their comfort zones.

For example, many are willing to accept particular forms of sickness, as mind manifested, but unwilling to see all forms of sickness, as mentally conjured. They instantly badger up and become incorrigibly reticent, if you even hint at this possibility. Nevertheless, their partiality on this should be rigorously questioned. Beneath it all, lies their unconscious insistence that the body still possesses some forms of intelligence. Still believing it is vulnerable to certain aspects of perception they will not bring this sacred cow to the marketplace just yet, to offer it up. Thus they cannot heal. They are fearful of a God who demands the sacrifice of all idols. However, Truth cannot hold any partialities, exceptions, preferences or limits. It does not make contingency plans, like your ego, does. Its sees no uncertainty ahead. Nor does it assign any hierarchical orders to illusions, knowing them all as unreal.

Once you become confident in your faith, will you know Truth has always surrounded you in every way — within and without! Then you will conceive of no order of difficulty to miracles. Only the doubting calculate and guard against uncertainties ahead because they have no essential trust in existence. Your conscious identifications are not at random. Thus you grasp tightly to certain familiar dream elements. You want these fragments of your idolatry to serve as a shield against an ominous threat you cannot perceive, but most certainly can feel.

Your ego investments in the body represent its last barrier and holdout. It craves this man-cave as a place to do its pleasure seeking and to entertain certain "special" friends. Without this sanctuary, it would feel naked and exposed.

For it would lose all access to its private worlds which it holds sacred. Without the body, all attachments would become instantly meaningless. Hence it demands you retain this solitary shrine to your self-made gods. Only so, can it continue to project all its poisonous, self-crippling thoughts to the screen of the world! Keep its dream alive! Any loss of faith in the body would undo it completely.

Meanwhile, Truth must seem like a nagging nanny because it seeks to dispossess you of all allegiances to the body. All the same, its motives are well-intentioned and pure. It simply wants to transport you quickly beyond the body's dark confines. Demonstrate that your existence is in no way contingent upon it. In fact, it knows the body is the only impediment to your creativity and seamless communication. Of course, Truth will never scare you. It knows you would be freaked out, if every time you looked in the mirror, you saw nothing there — just this vaporous cloud of light in which all worlds had been swallowed up. The body will not permanently disappear until you are ready.

In fact, because of the tremendous power of your past conditioning, it can't. This image has become deeply embedded in your memory, and it is from there that it is being projected. Very rigid imprints have been established, that will not be erased until you are ready to let them go. Thus the body will continue to show up in your perceptions, even after vision has clearly shown, it is not there. Like a phantom limb, it will prop its head sporadically from time-to-time but eventually not be remembered at all. As your vision strengthens, the body, and the world will disappear for more extended periods. Each will become more shad-owy and ephemeral, and this signifies your acceleration out of time.

THE EXPERT SWORDSMAN

Once in an ancient time, there lived an expert swordsman. One day, his services were requested to complete the decapitation of a captured king. The king's dying wish was for a final cup of tea before his beheading. This beverage he thoroughly enjoyed. Shortly afterward he complained about a headache. The swordsman giggled cynically and said to the king, *"You can't possibly have a headache because you no longer have a head."*

Yes, your body is this headache without a head. It has no steadfast reality, just an illusory one. It may still seem to exist, long after you have recognized through vision, that it is not there. However once this priceless jewel of your ego has fallen, even for a moment, you will never look at yourself, nor the world ever quite the same. Its eventual disappearance will not be a time of sadness and loss, but one of immense celebration because then you will have released the crown jewel of all ego interference.

You have never needed the body. In fact, it places a limit on your capacity to communicate and it undermines your ability to seamlessly indulge in the experience of Whole-Mind. As I related before:

"To be without a body, is to be in our natural

state."   **[WB72.9.3]**

Hence the body's demise is not your end, but your home-coming. It will bring you to that place of undisturbed peace and soul-soothing rest. Until then, it will always function smoothly and flawlessly wherever it is needed. Its health, invulnerability, and fathomless energy reserves are de-rived from your intimate connection to Spirit. When you no longer worship this ego idol of temptation and attack, its health will be maintained.

Once you use it to communicate truth exclusively, it will never be sick. There will come an instant when you are ful-ly healed of mind. Then the body becomes irrelevant. So ends the sad dream of sickness, time and separation. You may remember these words, I spoke :

"Perhaps you do not realize that this removes

the limits you had placed upon the body by the

purposes you gave to it. As these are laid aside,

the strength the body has will always be

enough to serve all truly useful purposes. The

body's health is fully guaranteed, because it is

not limited by time, by weather or fatigue, by

food and drink, or any laws you made it serve

before. You need do nothing now to make it

well, for sickness has become impossible."

[ACIM, WB.136.18:1-4]

YOGIS AND SAINTS, WHO OVERCAME THE BODILY ILLUSION

(Sharon) I find your teachings pertaining to the body's ephemeral nature fascinating, if not outright astonishing. They go unashamedly against everything taught in the modern age.

This sad depot is forever barking into our ears of our critical needs for food, shelter, nutrition and sex to survive. Endlessly preaching, that if we don't drink water or fluids for two days or more, we will die. That we need sunblock to protect ourselves and at least ten hours of sleep a night, or we will become grumpy and weary.

It goes on-and-on with its litany of sales pitches, bombarding us every moment with a plethora of meretricious panaceas for our pain. The catalog includes our bogus needs for various vaccines, inoculations, remedies, prescription drugs, vitamins, exercise, human growth hormones, steroids, transplants, and so on. Business is great, it seems, once you tie people to the body and do not let them free. Thus have arisen, all those emerging New Age fields catering exclusively to our holistic health including Naturopa-

thy, Allopathy, Homeopathy, Ayurvedic therapy, Bioener-
getics, Stem Cell Research, Reiki and so forth. It seems
there is no end to the chase after perfect health. Nonetheless, it remains as elusive, impermanent and mythical as
chasing the Crock of Gold, at the end of a rainbow. Then,
when you attest the exact opposite, it is like a real stab in
the dark to the dark powers that be — those predacious
merchandisers in sickness and instigators of fear. Can you
substantiate your declaration that we have no physical
needs?

(Jesus) I, myself, thoroughly exposed our independence of
all physical needs during my forty days spent in the desert.
When I resurrected and reappeared to the apostles, I perfectly demonstrated the powerlessness of the body over
the mind. Since the body is just a neutral learning device
that is mentally projected, it has no needs. You may ask
from where could all such unholy needs arise? Follow the
money, as always! Only those suckers, who take the external world to be real can believe in such foolishness!

Nevertheless, there are many great yogi's and saints down
the ages who in moments of deep meditation have seen by
means of naked perception the bodily illusion. By leveraging strict yogic and ascetic practices, they were able to by-

pass all evil positivistic and materialistic based beliefs. All insidious influences of modern society. One excellent example is Babaji, the Indian Yogi that continues to materialize wherever he is needed. He has reappeared many times in the last two millennia alone — most recently to the yogis S.A.A. Ramaiah and V.T. Nealakantan in the Himalayas in the1950s. Having overcome the illusion of the body, he has the Siddhi power to instantly appear anywhere he is needed.

He can also manifest any object of his desire, simply by focusing his undivided attention on it. He employs the Yoga of one-pointedness of mind, known as *Eka-Grata* and is one of the greatest Yogis who propagate higher understandings to open minds. He recognized that all seeming loss of mind-power was due to the conditioning influence of wrong beliefs. That the mind has a tendency to become inflexible, overly filtered and fixated when it is restricted to very band-limited horizons. By freeing himself from the static imprint of rigid and frozen beliefs, as well as from all attachments, he was able to become completely immersive in the present moment. As a vaporous and highly superconscious being; he has attained the mental dexterity and superfluity of mind demanded, to harness all natural creative powers.

Other yogis have had this power, including Atisha, Padmasambhava and Trailanga Swami. In fact, there is a multitude of yogis in India today who have gone without food and water for years on end without any adverse health issues. Some transmute pranic energy into nutritional energy. All, however, are derivations of mental energy, because that is the only creative force in existence. It can only be made truly creative when it has become spiritualized. Often these yogis will go naked on the glaciers without a care in the world and walk about for months in the dry summer heat without suffering sunburn or dehydration. They know all acute fluctuations and shifts in the global air conditioner are powerless over the virility of their thought. Trailanga Swami, to be abundantly honest, was a bit of an exhibitionist. He would go around naked and spend many days under the Ganges, near Benares without coming up for air. Also, he had the power to dematerialize his body at will. Therese Neumann needed no food for the last few decades of her life, since she had discovered her divine essence and knew this was what really sustained her.

Most dreamers however, are far too form-obsessed and creatively blind to manifest anything at all. They function more like pusillanimous beings who have lost all spiritual will and muscle. Nor are they open to the ways of wisdom and Knowledge. Even though awesome powers remain latent within them, they cannot leverage them and function more like monkeys with a keyboard. They buy in completely to the dream of the material world and believe whatever the media and popular culture blasts their way. You will see them plodding to the stores with credit cards in hand, not having the slightest clue how their food it produced or where it comes from. They will graciously imbibe all forms of toxic junk, GMOs, and harmful insecticides, as long as it is placed in an attractive wrapper and takes 30 seconds or less to microwave. Then they knock it all back by swilling down a half a dozen sugar spiked sodas or a case of beer. Then maybe they will indulge in a postprandial brandy or two, along with a fine cigar.

Then there are others, who perceived the unreality of the body through an out-of-body (**OBE**) or near-death experience (**NDE**). The triggering event is often a near fatal accident, an inoperable sickness, a mentally shattering episode or bout of intensive drug use. Having nothing to lose, they came fully into the present moment for the first time and saw through the very hypnotizing dream of their conditioning.

Even so, all that is needed to see through this illusion is a very heightened state of open and unbiased awareness. One in which all noise, distractions and attractions of the world are filtered out. Only then is the infinite given license to penetrate through to the mind and to provide the mystical vision of true Reality. Then one captures in an instant, that pure and formless space, that has always been.

Those few who are enlightened, abide fulltime in this extremely potent and timeless space. Availing of it, to refresh themselves and for entering into loving communion with the Holy One. It is clearly evident to the awakened, that all appearances of the body and of form arise out of ignorance, as do all phenomena in the dreamworld.

As I mentioned earlier, the body's seeming appearance is entirely due to memory and anticipation. It cannot exist wholly in the present moment because it has never been a part of Truth. Thus, one is always projecting the veil of one's beliefs and expectations over the present, which then causes the bodily illusion to appear. Memory is the holder of all imprints derived from one's mental convictions and past experiences. It is from memory that one's conditioned belief system arises. The body has a strong residual imprint there and its seeming appearance is but an effect of one's past conditioning.

Anticipation, implies that we always expect to see in the future that which we saw or experienced in our past. So one's future is manufactured entirely out of one's conditioned beliefs and wish-fulfillment desires. In effect we are always just seeing our past projected into the present and never the true present. Instead its purity and refulgence become lost in the perpetual haze of our conditioning.

Our very biased perceptivity and clumsy reaction times, are major obstacles that block truth from our awareness. Only those, who have attained to vision and enlightenment and so escaped the delusion and trickery of impure understanding can perceive the naked present.

> **"At no single instant does the body exist at all. It is always remembered or anticipated, but never experienced just *NOW*. Only its past and future make it seem real. Time controls it entirely, for sin is never wholly in the present."**
>
> [ACIM, T-18.VII.3:1-4]

OUR CONDITIONED AWARENESS AS AN IMPEDIMENT TO VISION

(Sharon) It seems our conditioned awareness is a chief obstacle to vision. Can you explain how it interferes with Truth?

(Jesus) Conditioned awareness always tracks what which is phenomenally present, rather than phenomenally absent. In other words. It is biased towards objects and phenomena and all that can be sensed and perceived. Thus it emphasizes, amplifies and exclusively focuses in on the phenomenal over the noumenal and ontic. Anything that is outside one's range of sensation or conception becomes quickly lost and unknown.

Take a bicycle wheel, for example. When it is motionless, one clearly sees the spokes and the spaces between them. However, as we rotate the wheel faster, all the spokes start blending together, and the spaces between disappear. Though the spaces are still present, they are not registered. This is exactly how the power of conditioning works in the mind, to perform all its magic tricks of deception and how it blinds us to true reality. With the bicycle wheel, all depends intimately on your reaction time, expectation and bias towards that which is phenomenally present. Consequently, even though empty space predominates, all you see is the blurred blending of the spokes.

Even so, high-frequency energy waves can readily and imperceptibly pass through the rotating wheel and appear on the other side. This is because the movement of the wheel is pretty stationary in comparison. So it is with all vibratory phenomena. Our awareness only tracks that which is moving in a certain range relative to our reaction time and all else is filtered out. That which is changeless does not catch our interest or attention. Neither do any phenomena beyond our narrow filters of sensation.

It is the nature of the relative mind, to be prejudicially focused on movement, form, and change over that which is formless and changeless. Thus, the eternal realm, though ever-potent realm gets filtered out because of its changelessness. We are continuously shaping the world of our perception into alignment with the matrix of our expectations and beliefs! For example, when the Spanish sailors first arrived in North America, the Native Americans could not see them. The reason being, we see predominantly with the eyes of our mind. However, this inner eye is intensely biased. It only captures that which it believes in and therefore expects. Since the natives had never seen ships, horses or strange-looking folk before, the lens of their conditioned expectation automatically filtered them from view. In effect, their inherent conditioning made them temporarily blind to important perceptual aspects present all about them. They had to train their minds to readjust and gradually expect such appearances before they could actually perceive them.

When I said that, *"The Father's Kingdom is spread out upon the earth, and people don't see it."* [Gospel of Thomas], I was referring to this power of conditioning. Most are too conditioned by their ego beliefs to see the divine all around them. They are incapable of naked perception. Instead each perceives a very rigid object-orientated universe of sharps contrasts and differentiations, as programmed from the template of their expectations and limited understandings. The vast network of ego defenses and fears they embrace only serves to make their world picture far more conditioned and narrow filtered.

Without all this nonsense, they would know unity and non-separation as a veritable fact — not just as a mere possibility. The power of your conditioned belief is what enlivens and enacts the dream of separation. You do not doubt what you perceive since it crystallizes out of your beliefs. I also taught you this in the Course. Here for example:-

"**This space you see as setting off all things from one another is the means by which the world's perception is achieved. You see something where nothing is, and see as well nothing where there is a unity; a space between all things, between all things and you. Thus do you think that you have given life in separation. By this split you think you are established as a unit which functions with an independent will.**"

[ACIM, WB.184.2:1-4]

Vision is the exact opposite of conditioning. It arises from being impartially honest and open-minded. It only emanates when you relinquish that gravely prejudicial belief system that currently molds your view. When you no longer cling to rigid incorrigible beliefs and narrow bands of thought, you will no longer distort. The net impact of all this is that the real is welcomed at last. Then emerge your pure and luminous perceptions, and this is known as naked perception.

(Sharon) So conditioned awareness is by nature narrow and prejudicial! **What particular prejudices, shape, and narrow-band our conditioned awareness?**

(Jesus) All erroneous beliefs do! Your reactionary impulses of fear and desire are particularly corrosive. Meanwhile, the poison of your many attachments and aversions twist your mind into becoming extremely judgmental. When your viewing matrix becomes profusely programmed by the ego's insidious content your neuroleptic brainwashing is complete. Then thoroughly infused, by genetic mind algorithms roaming riotously within, you succumb to the viral malware of the ego mind. Taken collectively, the matrix of one's temporal conditioning is what produces all illusions of separation.

Conditioning is highly influential. It molds and manipulates your mind into perceiving unreal hallucinations while rendering invisible that which IS.

As a consequence, the important gets rejected and filtered while the trivial gets amplified out of all proportion. So you place your mind in chains by holding it captive to a hallucinatory universe born from its own conditioning. A bleak unseemly universe arises, woven from the fabric of all your biases, partialities, exceptions and limits. Conditioning though having no power to create can nevertheless be very potent in its capacities to block and distort.

Your original rejection of God and the unconscious guilt that followed was the decisive element that made you both myopic and presbyopic. It was in that unholy instant that you first became partial. Before that, you embraced all, wholeheartedly and without question. You had no vested interests or unnatural agendas. Unconscious guilt serves, as the unholy basis that propagates all unrealistic fears and aberrant desires. In the haze of one's "conditioned" blindness, all idols and sacred cows suddenly gain in importance.

Most are mortally afraid to look at the original error of the **TMI** and its fatal consequences. Terrified they will lose all sanity, if they delve too deeply into the hallowed ground of the ego. Thus their minds are in great turmoil like a ship mercilessly tossed about by hundred foot waves off the

Cape of storms. This ship is our body, and the waves are our thought patterns. The ego, of course, is the captain who cruelly commands where the ship is going. It wants us to hold tight to this precious cargo of gems and trinkets. Preaching any hint of abandonment will sink us expeditiously to the bottom of the ocean and drown us in the sea of self-annihilation.

Each must realize that harboring nonsense beliefs mentally molds so that the real seems absent. Untruths do not cost one reality but they do cost awareness of it. One's prejudicial beliefs do work against one's own best interests by inhibiting vision and dimming recognition of one's eternal treasures. In the final analysis, what treasures do we need but unconditional Peace and Bliss! Peace, however, can never be found by those who entertain idols in its place. For who can find peace who simultaneously assigns value to the meaningless.

In the end, your choice is simple. You can have either truth or illusion, reality or dreams, awakening or sleep but never both together. This is the range of your choice and makes decision-making simple. God does not spread himself out into a vast array of endless and meaningless choices.

All paths lead to Truth once your motives are pure. Your interpretation of the path, is what is all-important because this is also how you will be viewing your own reality.

Look to underlying content, and your meager efforts will be monumentally rewarded. Then you will finally break the seal of illusion that surrounds your mind and bypass the dark conditioning power of false beliefs. Then the lotus, at the Sahasrara chakra will flower, and a thousand windows will open, offering you numerous fragrant portals to the infinite. All an ominous and portentous sign, that your consciousness has finally blossomed and that you have reached beyond the limits of the conceptual. Now you find your being infused with true life, versatility, and power.

When you no longer hold sacred unworthy attachments, judgments and fears, the imposing matrix of all your conditioned beliefs will melt easily away. Then you become free of time, because an impartial and unattached mind enters effortlessly to Truth. Having become incapable of distortion, the Real world opens up before you in its full panoramic splendor. Then you discover the Buddha-Mind within, who is the perfect creator and reflector of Truth and always Here-Now!

Until that glorious and fortuitous instant, you will not recognize His presence within because you will remain too obsessed with the time-bound, partial, unworthy and conditioned. The Buddha-Mind must always roam free in the timeless, whole, unconditioned, and limitless. Only so can it move unimpeded through all worlds, and recognize itself as their Source. Knowing itself only as that perfect inextinguishable awareness, which has no needs. There is nothing apart from the supreme One. No past or future, just an everliving present.

THE IDEATIONAL MATRIX THAT LEAD TO THE BODY

(Sharon) You have described some essential issues associated with having a bodily Identity. **However, there must be some causal chain of connectivity leading from our Eternal Home, to where we seem to find ourselves now?**

(Jesus) Our denial of God was the only cause of the relative existence. Denial led to all our problems. Before that, any experience of guilt was impossible. The Tiny-Mad-Idea (TMI), in particular, was the triggering event that seemed to cast us out of Heaven. Once we experienced guilt, we soon felt it tearing our minds apart. Our strongest desire was for immediate pain alleviation. However, the only known painkiller for guilt is innocence. Unfortunately, our innocence seemed totally out of the question.

The insatiable demon of our inner guilt produced the body to give us a taste of the innocence, we so deeply craved. There was only one cost. Our innocence would be illusory, and we would need to find scapegoats to preserve this illusion. Thus, giving our guilt to others was the bargain made!

We accomplished this by splitting and partitioning our Whole Mind into various bodies. Certain carefully chosen specimens would become targets for our guilt. All, so that the rest of our mind could live in peace. The plan was to bathe in the luxurious and soul-soothing sauna of our illusory innocence and ignore what was on the outside.

Meanwhile, all those "guilty" factions were excommunicated to live in those frozen Siberian wastelands, strategically positioned outside the fence of our bodies. Their sentence was never to be commuted through our forgiveness. Hence, we would keep projecting all our guilt thoughts in their direction. Anytime, they were up for parole; we would find something new, devious and scandalous to sentence them afresh. We could accuse them of vengeance, corruption, falsehood, mercilessness, murder, perversion, victimization, deception and so forth, all to keep them forever as a thing apart.

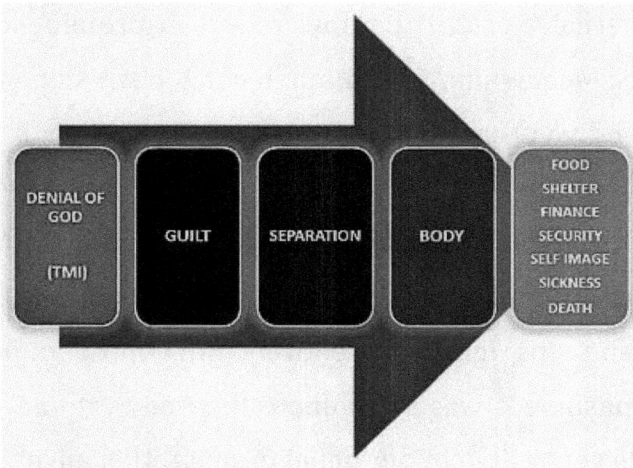

CAUSAL CHAIN LEADING FROM DENIAL AND THE TMI, TO THE BODY

Sin worked wonders because we could assign sins for just about anything we fancied. It was a pretty neat and snug arrangement and guaranteed to make their jail term permanent. Sin had many other advantages. Firstly, it amplified the importance of the body out of all proportion. Under the commandership of sin, the body became multifold in its purpose. It could be transformed into a den of entertainment, a vehicle of hate, a temple of innocence or a totem pole of our specialness. It was here in this home of our idolatry, that we first enshrined our ego's chosen deities to godhood.

Secondly, sin strengthened all our magical beliefs. By mentally assigning certain powers and capacities to aspects of the external world, it became raised in prominence and stature. Meanwhile, our mind having been demoted to serf-hood went into hiding. Every, now and then, it would raise its feeble voice, to say *"This should not be happening."* Alarmed, it would sometimes cry out **"Stop the Madness!"** But the world of bodies, poisoned by all its lusts, temptations, and sins, ignored it entirely. Sin's most impressive accomplishment was to promote the body into an incontestable verity. It kept our belief in separation alive.

To this day, our continued attraction to guilt and our complicity to magic keeps sin well nourished and beyond all doubt. It has become an idol to be worshiped but never questioned. One of our ego's favored Gods. We are attracted to it, like flies around dung. The only cure for our belief in sin was forgiveness, but this, we dared never mention in public. Forgiveness, seemed to demonstrate weakness and so like the leper in the family, was a thing of great shame. It would extract all the fun and mischief out of our lives and toss us to the side of the pavement to be ridiculed by the visceral and worldly. Rob us of all ego power and our commendable accomplishments in the name of separation.

We became afraid of extending peace and blessing to "others," in case all those artificial boundaries, established by sin would quickly disappear. Then finding no protection, we would be left at the mercy of our enemies. No! We must build more walls. We will continue our allegiances to sin, even if it means screaming out for yet more punishment and directing our minds to a future filled with fear and dread. Yes, we prefer to remain savagely conflicted within, rather than needlessly sacrifice our position of power. So, the coat of our misery is one well worn.

We really do believe that relinquishing sin demands sacrifices. That forgiveness would deprive and weaken us in the eyes of our enemies. However, all that will eventuate with the restoration of vision, is our divine inheritance will rise back into your awareness. Then finding the body purposeless, it will be fast expunged back into the nothingness from which it came.

Forgiveness serves to gently cleanse our minds of all beliefs in guilt. Doing so, it gradually rids us of all unnatural ego desires, including those for specialness, power, pleasure and attack. Because all such alien desires only arose in the vacuum of our lost innocence. Then, losing all interest in maintaining separation and at profiting at another's ex-

pense, we heal all boundaries and are restored to an illuminated state of mind. Forgiveness likewise unburdens us
of all self-made barriers that lead to sickness, isolation,
joylessness, and fear. It restores us to the recognition of
Unity and Whole-Mind. No aspect of the Sonship is to be
excluded or condemned. All are to be given their rightful
inheritance and seen to share fully in the Power,
Knowledge, and Sovereignty of our divine Source.

Nothing survives its purpose! This is the law that governs
the relative existence and is true of forgiveness as it is of
the body, guilt and sin. You would not see the body unless
you were investing there. So long as you believe, it has the
capacity to bring you lasting peace and joy, you will never
make the sacrifice of sin. This, however, blocks awareness
of your everlasting innocence. Forgiveness ends the dream
of guilt and this holy function is the Atonement.

THE MYTH OF OBJECTIVISM

(Sharon) The world today, is a cauldron of panic, sweat, and anxiety. A place of endless frustrations and so many complex demands. Persistent feelings of separation and isolation can often overwhelm us, at times. It is hard to deny our present picture of a very fragmented and meaningless universe because this is our very first-hand experience of living. Everywhere we go, the temptress is waiting, ready to hypnotize us with endless new fads, inventions, healing concoctions, and ingenious play-toys. Everyone seems distracted and taken in.

Even the concept of objective existence is considered an irrefutable fact by most. So much so, that it seems sheer

lunacy to deny it. The modern New Age marvels of consumerism, technology, medicine and genetics have temporarily blinded us. While they so freely and persuasively
thrive, any discussion of there being a possible metaphysical or spiritual basis for our existence, seems frivolous, un-
hip or even seditious.

**Apart from the TMI, what recent evolutions in thought
have led to this brainwashing?**

(Jesus) The modern facelift you are seeing now had its
genesis a few thousand years ago. It started with the ancient Greeks. Even though the Greek philosophers taken
collectively did extensive good, Aristotle himself effected
inordinate damage. Once he arrived on the scene, the
greater hub of humanity was sent careening down the
wrong path for two millennia. His pivotal work, *Organon*
lay the groundwork for our modern misplaced notions of
inhabiting a universe of separate things and forms.

He introduced and strengthened our belief in self-
contained "objects" which he regarded as fundamentally
concrete, hermetic and independent entities with implicit
self-natures of their own. His formal logic {**A = A**; and **A =
Not B**} reified "objects." From then on they were visualized

as entirely independent of their surroundings and only equivalent to themselves.

By further ascribing certain mysterious inner *essences* to objects, he enabled them to be envisioned as both self-powered and self-determining. In his mind, there was no *universal nature*, apart from the particular *essences*, he conceptualized as being inherent in each object. He then proceeded to strengthen the partitioning of the world further with his ideas on categories, levels, and orders. He certainly liked to have everything clearly labeled and neatly placed in its box. In his mind, the universe was a self-existing, orderly one and it functioned independently of our consciousness.

As a result, consciousness was given the back seat. It was no longer seen as the intelligent artificer of the world and quickly became relegated to its new role of a mere analyzer, sorter, and bookkeeper. If it could successfully crunch all the sense data it was incessantly bombarded with; it was given a bone. Because then it would apprehend those supreme *essences*, that composited the very fabric of the universe.

Nonetheless, the exact constitution or makeup of these *essences*, Aristotle never did quite reveal. Then universe to him was one of particulars, and everything had its class, rank, and file. There was not much room for the divine in Aristotle's scheme. His notion of divinity was that of an exogenous power whose domicile was the external world. To this end, he had proposed a fifth element Aether, which he conceived as being the divine substance that makes up the inner constitution of the stars and cosmos.

He emphasized the role of reason and logic exclusively, as humanity's indispensable tools for improving our position and better grasping the objective world of our perceptions. The inner world of mystical intuition had no real part to play in transferring divine knowledge to man. Thus with his arrival, the entire worldview had changed fundamentally for the worse. It soon became interpreted through an entirely fictitious framework. It was as if he had put a wire mesh over our world. An unnecessary encumbrance that created more walls between us and existence. This mesh was composed of all his theories, hypotheses, and categorizations and it fast became a distortive conceptual overlay through which we began to experience and interpret ourselves. Consequently, in one fell swoop of his metaphysical axe, he had seemed to reduce us all to mere prisoners of an objective universe.

All the excellent pioneering work of his predecessors, Anaxagoras, Socrates, Plato, Parmenides, Zeno, Xenophanes and so forth soon became buried in the dust. The outer world now became the primary focus of all investigations. So arose the new domains of Rationalism, Science and all Classical systems of thought.

(Sharon) Surely Aristotle did some good?

(Jesus) Some would claim he made spectacular accomplishments because he paved the way for many new stimulating fields to emerge including those of Computer Technology, Robotics, Cybernetics, Forecasting Systems and Intelligent Algorithms. In fact, any domain or specialty that attempts to improve upon itself, through deconstructionist approaches and enhancement of constituent components can be considered a descendent of Aristotelian thought. On the illusory level, at the very least, he unleashed a far more progressive universe of increased evolutionary capacities. His thought streamlined many new and exciting possibilities. Very few of our modern toys would have existed without him. We would still be galloping around in a horse and cart, without him. There would be no cruising the highways in our Lamborghinis. In this respect, he was akin to Father Christmas.

(Sharon) Still, I sense your doubt and sarcasm!

(Jesus) Aristotle was very much a man for the people, but not a man to champion the potency and latent Knowledge of Spirit. Gnostic insights and Revelatory experiences would be entirely lost on him. He doubted very much the existence of those intuitively felt worlds beyond the visible. In fact, he didn't even care for any reductionist approaches to the observed world. In contrast, he was enamored by increasing complexity and division. It was always a case of WYSIWYG with Aristotle. In short, he was the pure Philistine and the Joe six-pack of philosophers. The prevailing source of all the damage he inflicted was driving us deeper into the wormhole of unnecessary contrasts and artificial separations. So each entered an immensely partitioned universe of illusory boundaries from which they could never hope to escape or find any meaning.

Anaxagoras, in contrast, saw the mind (*Nous*) as the only force that moved the universe. He recognized that all forms and phenomena in the observed universe were inextricably bound and interconnected and part of an eternal substance which was non-differentiated and pure. He understood that it was this subtle and indistinguishable presence that possessed all power. That it was the kernel of the visible world and the incomprehensible.

Socrates, in turn, had directed us to the inner world of mind and thought. To him, it was futile, to attempt to grasp the outer world of appearances without first understanding oneself. In his view, all worldly knowledge was inherited, counterfeit and impure. Therefore suspect from the very beginning. He sought to uncover deeper metaphysical insights and universal truths by asking provocative questions. He made use of syncretic approaches to reconcile any contradictions, unearthed.

So he went about rigorously challenging all the wise people of his day. He soon found out, that their so-called wisdom did not hold up to scrutiny. The validity of their beliefs, once exposed, were either of limited scope or completely fallacious. Being immensely aware of his own innate ignorance, he saw uncertainty, as the path to wisdom and certainty, as the sure path to blindness. He can be likened to Lao Tzu in this manner, just as Aristotle can be favorably compared with Confucius. Socrates saw the "seen" world, as one of shadows and a mere proxy standing in for the real world of light. One could never hope to understand it by examining and analyzing its shadows because these chimerical apparitions of mind only arose from our own imperfect understandings. Once we gained access to the all-knowing light existing behind consciousness, all would be understood. This was our one hope of curing ourselves and reaching the perfection of the Gods. Plato then sought to hammer out and expound these profound teachings further, as seen in his *Allegory of the Cave*. Plato also taught of a universal essence; that was independent of all particulars and forms.

Zeno's unique method of knowledge exploration also stood in stark opposition to that of Aristotle. He liked to create riddles and paradoxes that exposed the fallacies and biases of our commonsense assumptions. For example, he revealed the paradox of a universe of separate things in his sage statement, "*If being is many, it must be both like and unlike, and this is impossible, for neither can the like be unlike, nor the unlike like.*" So this simple question was asking "*how does being procreate that which is unlike itself?*" Since it cannot bestow attributes, talents, and capabilities it does not intrinsically possess within itself.

There are only two possibilities. **(1)** *Being is unitary and indivisible, and all perceived differences are unreal* or **(2)** *Unified Being does not exist, and the universe is composed of a multiplicity of separate beings, disconnected objects, and phenomena, that have no real relationship or dependence upon one another.* The second is the Aristotelian worldview, and yet Avant-Garde findings in quantum physics clearly demonstrate; this is not so. In particular, Bell's Theorem and the experiments conducted on non-locality provide damning evidence against the Aristotelian view.

Similarly, Zeno's paradoxes of *The Arrow* and *The Tortoise and Achilles* are an assault on our very complacent objective beliefs in time and motion. These paradoxes controvert our conventional notions that time and motion are objective and continuous in nature. Kurt Gödel came later to present, his now famous *Incompleteness Theorem*. He too, with one fell swoop of his axe had proven that the Aristotelian system of logic could never be proven true and complete. Because any system of axioms and logic, even if 100% consistent, must still contain at least one premise or statement, that cannot be proven veracious from within its own context.

In the Aristotelian System, the inherent deficiency or false statement is clear. It is his original premise that **A = A;** and **A = Not B**. The same one, that proudly declares the world of separation and independence to be true. The deeper more incisive understanding is in recognizing, **all which appears to exist depends intimately on that which seems to exist not.** This is the fundamental mechanism of how the relative world maintains its illusion and mirage. Nothing can prevail in isolation and Aristotle's mythical object-orientated universe has no real framework on which to support itself. It is simply a magician's trick and delusional. If focuses on differences, while ignoring similarities.

Even so, there has never been even a single shred of evidence of any object, phenomena, or concept existing in absolute isolation. All the attributes that lend an object or phenomena its seeming existence and definition depend intimately on all its phenomenal interactions and relationships with its surroundings. Even that which remains unseen and so appears to be not can extend its influence to shape the world of appearances. The correct statement Aristotle should have made is **A = Both A and NOT A;** Since each so-called object is equivalent to itself, but also shares an intimate dependency, on all it appears to be not. Its surroundings work to maintain the mirage of its illusory presence.

Alexander the Great was the perfect student for Aristotle and seems to have imbibed his philosophy completely. He advanced it in his military campaigns and strategies of conquest. His not so subtle approach to unraveling the famed Gordian knot was to slice it open with his sword. This divide-and-conquer approach is exactly what Aristotle had done before him to the world of our perceptions. It is one of attempting to increase understanding through increasing separation. One of searching for higher meaning by first fragmenting and discombobulating all into meaningless parts.

Nonetheless, just as a beautiful woman will no longer retain her beauty, if you insist on plucking out her eyes and severing her limbs, likewise this approach does not work. The efficacious remedy involves unitary and holistic thinking. It is this that heals all beliefs in apparent separation.

ARISTOTLE'S MISCHIEVOUS COHORTS

(Sharon) Aristotle can hardly be held accountable for all the impact and damage. How about Euclid, Archimedes, Newton, Leonardo Da Vinci and so many others?

(Jesus) Alexander was the one who planted the tree that launched firm belief in a classical world of separation. Euclid and Archimedes came later. They helped market and launch Aristotle's core philosophy and can be considered part of his backup band. Together all three made a successful coup on world thought that lasted over two millennia.

Euclid was certainly sneaky. Through his axioms on spatial geometry, he helped cement the false notion of a dimensional universe firmly into place. This monumental feat of deception, he accomplished by inventing a mystifying array of hypothetical entities. First, he introduced the point and made it large enough, so that all could clearly see it. Then when he shrank it, to be infinitely small, all remained convinced that it was still there and a real, rather than hypothetical entity.

Then he extended this point infinitely to concoct the line, the line infinitely to form the plane and the plane infinitely to establish our current illusion of a real 3-dimensional space. So what arose from pure mental conjecture was consequently taken to be fact. Then this slick magician pointed to the "objects" in this space and convinced many that these objects were objectively there, rather than mere mirages of mind.

It all seemed to be good common sense knowledge. However, what is often deemed to be self-verifying, can often reveal the greatest lies. Euclidian space remains entirely hypothetical. Since no real point exists, neither does objective space. Unfortunately, some mathematicians began to take Euclid's theory seriously and advanced this mind-game a few stops further. Soon we began to buy-in also to higher dimensional spaces and unseen universes. Various string theories and concepts of expanding universes began to proliferate to bewitch the modern mind even more. We quickly forgot all these entities remained invented constructs, projected to the world of our perceptions. Instead, we transposed them into actualities.

(Sharon) Yes, but we can all feel 3-D objects in our hands, and the tactile sensations and impressions, we get, certainly makes us feel that they are objectively there and very real. **It is only natural that we also believe, the world we perceive is external to our minds.**

(Jesus) Yes, many convince themselves that such sensations are derived from an external object. They fail to see that sensation is a mental process. That it is the projection of their innate inner sensory capability that is producing the illusion of this object. The six inner sense indriyas that effect the illusion of objective existence are in turn programmed by the vast network of our past conditioning, expectations, and beliefs. Apart from this, no world would appear in one's perception.

A BOUGHT JURY

(Sharon) If this is so, why do so many remain unconvinced?

(Jesus) Their egos get in the way, and the ego is incapable of attaining to mystical vision and experiencing reality directly. It is not sufficiently empowered to ever see with naked perception because it lacks knowledge. It will, therefore, feel compelled to ideate various fanciful interpretations to explain the world it perceives. The ego, like Alexander wants to use its sword of judgment to carve up an entire world of separation. It hopes in the resulting chaos, and confusion you will lose your way and forget what the real questions were. The gazillions of different objects and phenomena you see and take to be real have been carved out of ego thought distortions. You do not recognize them as miscreations propagating out of your spiritual ignorance and driven by the power of your thought.

Similarly, you must grasp, that all those who believe in the physical universe are already biased towards inventing various hypothetical entities and mental constructs that serve to reinforce their beliefs. So they license their egos to work overtime building oceans of symbols and ideograms to represent all the strange images and impressions that flood their perceptions. They then like to play games of manipulation with these symbols and to build complex hierarchical overlays of abstraction into the world of illusion. All of which keeps you soundly mesmerized and looking in the wrong direction. Nevertheless, it is impossible to extract wisdom from the senseless. It is just as futile as selling ice to the Eskimos. Like I said in the past:-

"You live by symbols. You have made up names for everything you see. Each one becomes a separate entity, identified by its own name. By this you carve it out of unity. By this you designate its special attributes, and set it off from other things by emphasizing space surrounding it. This space you lay between all things to which you give a different name; all happenings in terms of place and time; all bodies which are greeted by a name."

[ACIM, WB.184.1:1-6]

Nonetheless, if a context is valid and real, it must be capable of providing proof of its validity from within itself. It must furnish, one quantity or premise, at the least that is beyond all doubt. If it cannot produce evidence of its self-efficiency from inside itself, its game is up! The incompleteness theorem has proven that so such system exists in the world, nor will one ever exist there. The world, like all formal systems based on symbols, premises and axioms will always hold at least one premise or belief that depends on external verification for its support. Consequently proof of the objective validity of the spacetime existence cannot ever be self-established.

THE HANDS OF THE MAGICIAN

(Sharon) Apart from yourself, are there any other sages who have seen through the deception?

(Jesus) If a lie is big enough, it will often be accepted as Truth. This is the cost of not looking, at where the magician is placing his hands. As you can see, the dark power of blindly accepting the hypothetical point rapidly spread its deception far beyond the world of our direct sensory experience. It soon unleashed prodigious ideations pertaining to "higher" mythical dimensions. After all, if we can be so easily tricked by our senses into believing in this world of appearances, why stop there? So, one well-placed lie can swiftly have stunning consequences.

Very few have seen through the deception. Most remain severely hypnotized sleep-walkers who buy-in completely to the myths of objectivism, separation, and the spacetime existence. The Buddhist Patriarch, Hui Neng was one Enlightened Master who escaped the deception. You may recall his simple, clear and powerful statement *"**From the first, not a thing IS.**"* It is the statement of one who has attained to wisdom and seen through all the charades projected by split-mind.

THE POWER OF INTERPRETATION

(Sharon) What difference does it make whether we continue to see the world as external and objective or realize instead that it is entirely projected? It seems our underlying experience will remain much the same!

(Jesus) In the beginning, there will be no real difference in your experience. Your conditioned expectations will still drive the universe of your perception and continue to determine what temptations will attract and dazzle you. So progress is glacial at first!

However, once you fully grasp that all appearances are mind-generated and arise out of ego endorsed beliefs, momentous and far-reaching changes becomes triggered into action. Once you cognize that there is no outer space, you comprehend simultaneously that the body and all its organs cannot exist as physical realities. Thus there is no real home for sickness to abide in. All forms of disease must, therefore, be the result of mental miscreation into the body. You produce such appearances, as a defense against Truth. It is your ego's inertia to change; that attracts your mind to beliefs in vulnerability. After all, if you are mortal, you cannot be divine. With this thought, the ego no longer feels threatened. Another consequence of your mental shift is that death is now recognized as an illusion. One you actively call for, whenever you are tired of the ego and its gifts. Likewise, all forms of space-travel become a joke. You see clearly now that you are always merely voyaging inside your own mind and thought.

This crucial shift enables you to approach the Godhead and peek at the real metaphysical foundations of the world. You begin to ask *"Does this Spacetime Artifice have a Purpose or is merely an Inconvenience?"* Your ego's purposes for it were many and included making Quixotic adventures to distant galaxies searching for new life-forms. The ego sees it as a pleasure seeking haven, and a place to engage in Mafioso style racketeering. So can it indulge its games of specialness and power! Now, you have an epiphany and honestly assess whether it may have a higher purpose. You begin to entertain the possibility, of its being just a learning device of the mind. One designed to heal you of your immense inner confusion. An abode where you can rid yourself of all strange ego beliefs, so that you can return to experiencing your Heavenly existence.

Thus, spacetime is interpreted correctly as that spiritual expedient needed in much the same way as a crutch by the lame. It presents an interim halting site where your current conceptual understandings can be evolved back into harmony with Truth. It soon becomes apparent, in this higher understanding that spacetime is a holodeck you are actively making, rather than one arbitrarily inflicted upon you against your will. You can use your experiences here strategically to navigate your way to light. All symbolic thinking modes are outpourings from the lower mind and represent ego attempts at demystifying this imaginary world of separation. One is not to get too caught up in ego symbols and concepts since they can be used very insidiously to reinforce this false world.

Everything, we perceive here has a higher meaning and function when used under the guidance of the Holy Spirit. Our experiences can restore our sanity and usher back awareness of our unassailable Divine Identity. Maybe, you can recall the following:-

> **"Use all the little names and symbols which delineate the world of darkness. Yet accept them not as your reality. The Holy Spirit uses all of them, but He does not forget creation has**

one Name, one meaning, and a single Source
which unifies all things within Itself."

[ACIM, WB.184.11:1-3]

**(Sharon) Does this imply that there are no such thing
as higher dimensional universes?**

(Jesus) There has never been even a single universe! This
essential understanding was echoed many times in the
Course. Here is just one example:-

"There is no world! This is the central thought
the course attempts to teach. Not everyone is
ready to accept it, and each one must go as far
as he can let himself be led along the road to
truth. He will return and go still further, or
perhaps step back a while and then return
again."

[WB.132.6:2-5]

All the same, higher dimensional universes do exist in the landscape of illusion. Such universes are not physically real in any way, but serve as reflections of a more evolved consciousness. They are projections of its heightened capacities for dealing with abstract and generalized thought-forms.

LAO TZU AND CONFUCIUS

(Sharon) Earlier, you compared Socrates to Lao Tzu and Aristotle to Confucius. This analogy seems to me rather oblique. **Can you briefly outline the baseline differences between Lao Tzu and Confucius's core philosophies to help me understand your comparison?**

(Jesus) Lao Tzu was a sage, who penetrated everything to its core. He loved to dive deep into the subaqueous realms and was not interested at all in the world of surface appearances. He knew, that which is at the surface comes and goes, but that which is at the depths remains forever. Once one becomes wise to the world, a state of extreme disillusionment must kick in. The closer one comes to wisdom, the more one's state of uncertainty increases. That is why Socrates had said, "*I know only one thing for sure, and that is I know, that I know nothing!*" Lao Tzu had reached this immense state of uncertainty too!

However, Lao Tzu had one slight problem — it was Confucius. Confucius was one to put lipstick on the pig. So his whole focus was in dressing up this world of superficial knowledge. In his vanity, his principal goal was to carve sense out of its senselessness. Unfortunately, his ideas began to spread virally. Soon everything had changed radically for the worse. Government authority grew enormously and began regulating every aspect of daily life. His vision was of hierarchical systems instantiating rule and order from the top down. So every day, new legal statutes, morality codes, values and virtues were being drawn up and enshrined as pillars of the modern state. An overly elaborate and convoluted system of checks and balances was expeditiously put into place, along with a very evil caste system. Before long, everything and everyone became quickly barcoded, tagged and bagged and placed into tidy little boxes.

Yes, Confucius was most certainly a control junky, laced with OCD, who wanted to implant various artificial forms of order into the chaos, he perceived. He desired to tame and sedate the tiger of existence. No one was trusted to be themselves anymore even on simple things like going about their business! The state possessed supreme power. Each was to know their position, boundaries, and limits and expected to behave with utmost dignity and servile deference to the new regime. Almost overnight, all had become prim and proper slaves to the *New World Order*. Any who disagreed were tarred and feathered, excommunicated and killed or humbled into lowly positions.

Lao Tzu was positively disgusted. He could not understand this burdensome tightening up and zealous overregulation of every aspect of daily life. He was mystified and perplexed by all the new fanatical obsessions with the phenomenal world. Did any still have eyes to see? Could they not recognize that all phenomenal appearances arose from an elusive unmanifest void that is supremely potent and undifferentiated? Could they not grasp that all these new hierarchies, restrictions, and orders held the very seeds to their own degeneration? That these cruel measures were suffocating the very life, they were intended to nourish and support?

All the newly emerging categorizations, quantifications, labeling schemes, repressions, and conformities would only ever provide an illusion of control and power. Their net effect would be to suck the lifeblood from all and extinguish the morale of the people. Nor could they ever hope to tame and subjugate that silent, invisible spirit that is the seed essence and power behind all! From the beginning, nothing was ever separate. All was intimately interdependent. The healing power, in which all flourished, depended on unimpeded communication and the smooth flow of knowledge — not the introduction of more barriers and rigorous formalities.

Lao Tzu, alone, seemed to realize the colossal damage that was being done and had taken the holistic view. He had the boundless vision to see the reality beyond. Sadly, he had grown old and weary of those around him. All were so small-minded and superficial. It was fast becoming a zombified world of the blind and psychologically crippled. He became totally sickened and nauseated by it all and like Pontius Pilot just wanted to wash his hands of the whole affair.

So he said, "I am done with this show, for now! I am tired of speaking to deafened ears. I am heading out into the desert to end my days." Even this was denied him. When he got to the gates, the sentry guard, who was posted there said, "*Hey, Greybeard, you have been eating our rice and corn for eighty years, fattened your belly on the meat of our pigs and probably raped our women. You're an entirely worthless being. Unless you give me a good bribe, I will not let you pass!*"

To this Lao Tzu responded, "*I come with empty hands and an open heart! There is nothing in that kingdom, that I cared for or desired to take. It is a lost and empty world to me. Everything I truly need is already within, where it has always been, as it is within you!*"

The commander quickly interjected, "*Listen now, that will not do at all! Don't flatter yourself! You must head over there to that shed and write some words of wisdom down, at the very least.*"

To this Lao Tzu quickly retorted, "*Words, words, words! That is all you ever care about. It is your perennial obsession and passion — along with seeking base pleasures, minor indulgences, and various perversions. What is wrong with you people? Can you not see that all words, symbols, concepts, and phenomena are unrealities? They can give no real nourishment, lasting joy or satisfaction! Akin to eating the recipe for a fine dish, in place of the meal itself. Following their endless dictates without effecting any inner change is about as efficacious as writing letters in the ocean. They are the last illusory sanctuary of the ignorant. Yet, you continuously immerse yourselves in them and smack your lips together in self-righteous conceit.*"

Thus it was, that two hours later he emerged from the shed, saying "*Here are your words Captain, but remember truth and wisdom, I cannot impart. Those jewels you will need to find for yourself by diving deep within. Also, one last thing, before I go! Could you give me one quick blast of the Hookah pipe?*" The Sentry guard looked at the transcript and his attention alighted on the following words, which pleased him immensely.

"Since before time and space were,

the Tao is.

It is beyond IS and IS Not.

How do I know this is true?

I look inside myself and see."

[Tao Te Ching]

SPACE-TIME AS A LEARNING DEVICE

SPACE-TIME, THE TUNNEL TO NOWHERE

(Sharon) What is the Relationship between Time and Space?

(Jesus) They are both two faces of the same illusion. Space is that aspect of the spacetime illusion present in your immediate field of awareness and "time" is reserved for that, not currently active in your thought. Being out of your awareness, it does not appear yet in your perception. Ultimately the entire matrix of spacetime already exists complete inside your mind. As I said before:-

> **"For time and space are one illusion, which takes different forms. If it has been projected beyond your mind you think of it as time. The nearer it is brought to where it is, the more you think of it in terms of space."**

[ACIM, T-26.VIII.1:3-5]

(Sharon) Why do we experience the Spacetime Illusion?

(Jesus) Once Knowledge became lost, you become incapable of assimilating the whole directly. This penalized you to operating through that split mode of mind, known as consciousness. Your conscious mind is incapable of grasping Truth in its Totality. Instead, it is dull, slow, and this limits your capacity to receive. So, does the whole, seem to become split into myriad frames! These frames then present their underlying content and veracities to you in various imaged forms, suited and adjusted for your limitations!

Your illusions of motion, change, birth, and old age are all introduced by your incapacities to imbibe Truth, in its entirety. All such appearances are produced from retaining errors and contradictions in your self-understanding. Because erroneous thought automatically distorts all your perceptions. As you divest yourself of all error prone thought, you heal your split-mind and become capable of apprehending the whole directly. Then the illusion of spacetime disappears, and the everpresent and changeless is once again evident.

In the meantime, these errors and contradictions handicap you, in every conceivable manner. They establish the special matrix of beliefs that shapes and forms your world. All the limitations in your psychic-evolutionary apparatus become projected to fashion the particular spacetime illusion, you now witness.

The ultimate understanding is recognizing your past, present, and future lives are all being lived simultaneously. Unfortunately, you are profoundly unconscious of them all. All the same, they continue to shape all your thoughts and emotions and mold your very being and destiny. Each of your probable selves exists parallel to you right now, like the ghost of Christmas past peering over your shoulder.

Each silently advises you to undo the mythical and beastly images you have self-created and projected into this relative kingdom of nowhere.

All your ego decisions and greater conditioning are powerless to mute the greater Voice within. They cannot block your alternate selves from influencing your awareness. There has never been any past or future, just qualitative changes happening in your awareness. Time is a psychically propelled illusion, generated out of your own endogenous state of conscious evolution. A diminished awareness, and you cannot remember what you had for breakfast. As your consciousness purifies and transmogrifies, you will remember all your lives. Whole-Mind is intrinsically motionless, perfect and transparent. As your unconsciousness becomes conscious, its wisdom becomes revealed.

(Sharon) How can I heal myself of all Errors and Contradictions?

(Jesus) Obscuring ignorance is the soil in which all contradictions thrive. It is the product of two antipodal beliefs systems competing for dominance, in the fabric of your thought. Your failure to wholly endorse the thought system of Truth exclusively, places you in a state of uncertainty and darkness. Believing in the power of darkness, the light within becomes blocked from shining outward into the world of your perceptions. So you fast lose sight of your original perfection and remain in a state of displacement from your true Self. The consequence of this is your firmly entrenched belief that you are some "body," hopelessly trapped in the confines of the spacetime existence.

(Sharon) Is Spacetime the only Illusion we Experience?

(Jesus) It can be considered the foundational basis in which all other illusions survive and proliferate. Motion and change are also illusory. All outer movement just mirrors your mind's deep state of confusion. For example, the great Buddhist Patriarch, Hui Neng was once asked, *"What causes a flag to move in the wind? Was it the flag or the wind?"* He humbly responded that it was merely the internal movements of the mind that caused the flag to move. The wise know that all movement is thought's reflexive action imprinted into perception. Nevertheless, fools will always react to apparitions formed from their own miscreative thought. So long as the mind remains impure, conceptually limited and bound to the beliefs of darkness, it will continue to experience the spacetime illusion.

Think of your consciousness as sucking on the ocean of Truth through a straw. Taking in the higher reality, as a series of 3-D fragments or slices but never experiencing the whole ocean directly. The illusion of spacetime is that which ingresses through the straw. It presents a veritable cocktail of esoterica that keeps you dazzled, consumed and bound to a world that is not there. Even so, this world could be dissolved completely in one revelatory moment of higher thought. This will transport you in an instant, through a quantum leap in your psychic-evolution.

(Sharon) So you see Spacetime as our Training Wheels and the result of our Psychological Limitations?

(Jesus) Yes, your mind and its beliefs are the sole causal agent of the world you perceive. Your spacetime illusion is being driven by your psychological states. These trigger certain portions of a higher dimensional construct to come into view which then unfold as a series of pictures, better known as your life. Nonetheless, you have never been embedded in spacetime, rather it is spun from within you, like the web from a spider.

In truth, nothing has even happened. However, subtle and important shifts in your beliefs trigger changes in how you perceive the undifferentiated Oneness. You are always just glimpsing that which is whole, pure, omnipotent and immaculate from a slightly different angle. All illusions of change and motion are brought on by imperfections in your own viewing apparatus. Once you purify the template of your mind, by purging it of all incorrect beliefs and inconsistencies, all seeming outer motion and events will come to an end.

At present, you cannot recognize the meaningful relationships inherent in all. You just see a cruel mosaic of random and disconnected fragments. You cannot capture, nor understand how all the elements come together to form a far greater picture. As your conceptual understandings evolve into alignment with truth, the straw of your consciousness will no longer be needed. Then you can toss it away because you will have reached the supra-conceptual understanding that transcends the world of form.

Each of your lives, it is like you are renting videos from a large cosmic library. This library is already complete, like the great library of Alexandria, before it was destroyed. All the videos in this library represent hallucinations of your own ego thought. As you watch the videos and make the necessary corrections, their illusory aspects begin to disappear. Hence, the only real change, ever happening, is in your awareness of truth. The transparency alone is changing. These videos are your key learning tool to take you to truth and merely reflect your current instantaneous learning needs. Your decisions and progress determine which ones you will need to watch next.

(Sharon) How is Spacetime best used as a Learning Device?

(Jesus) Spacetime only ever reveals changes in your conscious evolution. Distortionary beliefs are the cause of all that is illusory. Collectively, the nexus of your pet beliefs functions as an imprisoning overlay over your pure state of Mind. This overlay is all that prevents you from witnessing Truth directly.

The aim of all learning is to successfully clarify, resolve and eliminate incorrect understandings so that their illusory effects, no longer show up in your perception. This purification process can rapidly release whole sections of the past and future. Any correction made, heals your mind both retroactively and progressively. Ultimately this process removes the need for perception altogether. Each and every moment, you are being presented with a picture that images your maximal learning potential, for that particular moment in time. You can accelerate this purification process immeasurably by dropping all beliefs in guilt. Guilt triggers that vicious cycle of separation, fear, judgment, and defensiveness. As a result, your mind morphs into a black hole, from which no light can ever escape.

The ego and its thought survive through guilt, and this, in turn, justifies all its unfortunate attitudes, investments and behaviors. If you invest in guilt, you will be denied vision and therefore rendered incapable of healing. Nor will you be able to witness the many miracles in which Reality becomes apparent. Guilt extends your passage in time. Choosing guilt-based decisions is like getting to the local store via Antarctica. Guilt directs you through the spacetime matrix along that path that leads furthest from the light. So you get caught-up for countless millennia in various cul-de-sacs of the spacetime fabric. Timelessly trapped in dark conduits of thought where counseled exclusively by the ego you just spin your wheels in hopeless frustration.

Once all attraction to guilt is dropped, your spacetime journey comes rapidly to an end. The full extirpation of guilt from your mind is the only purpose of quantum forgiveness. As you begin to relinquish guilt, you are given the VIP treatment and released of all space-travel anxieties. Released of all self-defeating and toxic ego thoughts, you start to look forward to the journey. Your need for vengeance and attack having subsided, you relax and embrace your remaining Dreamtime adventure. So begins the happy dream that presages your imminent awakening.

No longer tempted by vain ego idols, you begin to enter the true present. Almost immediately, your capacity to work miracles vastly proliferates. As all dark videos disappear from your mind, the new holomotion picture becomes one of luminous and joy-filled experiences. Now you begin to understand why nothing ever happens at random. Each event was a call for your healing and arose from that deeper part of your mind, which just wants to go Home.

Spacetime has always been entirely neutral yet it can go on almost forever unless you make critical changes in your self-understanding. Alternatively, it can be employed masterfully to escape the dream of the relative existence.

(Sharon) It seems our Temporal Voyage is not Linear at all, as we are made to Believe?

(Jesus) Time has never been linear or continuous. As your mind gains in evolutionary momentum, time dilates. Have you never noticed this before? In those moments, when you are most self-aware, time slows down. Then, when you become lost in some menial tasks and engaging foolish obsessions, hours can go by without you noticing their passing. It is the gaps in your awareness that create the illusory experience of time. When your awareness is complete, time will come to an absolute standstill. For example, suppose you are involved in a crash on the highway, you will notice your awareness has suddenly become intense and everything is seen in slow motion.

(Sharon) Yes, I observed this for myself, just the other day. My attention was distracted for less than a second, during which time the car ahead abruptly came to a halt. A part of my mind then snapped responsively into action, and I avoided smashing into the other car by inches. Now I have a mental video of the full event stored away forever, even though it lasted just a few seconds.

(Jesus) You noticed that time dilated for you, but did the time-sense likewise adjust for a casual observer nearby? So maybe now you have a glimpse into the psychological nature of time and its relationship to your awareness. Similarly, when you go bungee jumping from bridges, the complete free-fall may last just a few seconds, but for you, it can seem to take forever. You get that sensation of being frozen in time, as you plunge mercilessly towards the ravine and its enormous boulders.

In all moments of high stress or during unexpected events, we can feel lifted out of the time illusion. It is only then we see it for what it is. Such events represent temporal discontinuities or points of inflection in the dream of time. At a temporal discontinuity, the time illusion is completely broken, and a point of inflection one experiences temporal dilation.

During the greater section of your life, there may be nothing very fascinating, freaky or exotic enough happening to capture your attention. Nothing to grab your focus and make you more aware. This can condition you into believing time is uniform, continuous and self-existent. Awareness only increases in those moments, for which we have no past reference in our memory banks. That is during any new or emerging situation, for which we have no pre-programmed routine or habit for automatically dealing with it.

However, most move through life like automatons or unconscious machines. Functioning through all those canned routines they have for dealing with life's exigencies. Their sleep of unconsciousness is so great that the Buddhas have said we are all fast asleep with our eyes open.

(Sharon) I remember one time driving back from New England, with a working companion. We had been lumberjacking all morning in the intense heat and now were immensely fatigued. As we were barreling down the hwy at ~ 80mph, suddenly our truck veered right off the road and down an embankment. Two of the tires were thoroughly shredded, and we were lucky to escape with our lives. I had thought my friend was awake since his eyes had been partially open, but in fact, he had really been asleep at the wheel. I guess this is just a sample of how we move through our lives, most of the time.

(Jesus) Yes, most drift unconsciously about for their entire lives. Then it is over before they know it.

(Sharon) Many still believe in objective time. For example, NIST defines one second very rigorously as *"The duration of 9 192 631 770 periods of the radiation corresponding to the transition between the two hyperfine levels of the* *ground state of the cesium 133 atom."* Others will point to their atomic clocks if you even hint that time is psychological and subjective in nature. It seems their arguments are legally incontestable.

(Jesus) This definition is based on a known burst of radiation based on two discrete events. Nonetheless, one cannot use the discrete to prove the reality of that, which is supposedly continuous. Because, between any two discrete events, its presence and continuity finds no witnesses. So it cannot be assumed to be continuous and present. Lifetimes could easily go by between any two such events, and there would be nothing there to mark or delineate this.

Once you slow down time through developing an increased awareness, you will begin to see this for yourself. Then the two discrete events of the cesium atom will be seen to be standing still.

(Sharon) I do not need to increase my awareness to dilate time. I could just take the individual frames of a favorite movie, then randomly reassemble them and watch the film over and over, as a personal punishment. By de-linearizing the script and so opening up the highly filtered processes of our thought, the same movie would then seem to take forever.

(Jesus) The time-dilation, you experience is due to changing the variable of your conditioned expectation. The correct understanding is knowing that the time-sense is always relative to one's psychological state and level of awareness.

THE TIME MACHINE

(Sharon) There has always been the wish for a time machine. How wonderful, it would be to slow down time at the pleasurable and critical moments in life — or even to stop the clock entirely. It would be nice to revisit some previous blunders and undo them or to rethink some stock purchase decisions. Imagine being able to make a week of vacation last forever. More time to spend with the important people in your life and for seizing emerging opportunities. Stress and anxiety would also be incalculably reduced, if not eliminated. Communication would be enhanced, since you would always have a witty response on the ready, instead of some clumsy, inarticulate nonsense.

(Jesus) This time machine already exists inside you, because you are the spinner of time. Time derives entirely from your ego thoughts. Before the ego crept in, time was completely unneeded and unknown. The ego keeps you threaded to time through guilt, fear, and desire. As you purge yourself of all ego thoughts, you will reenter the timeless dimension. To the extent that you do so, the vertical portal of the Eternal will open up before you and be self-evident, once more.

Simply drop all your future obsessions and thoughts of taking vengeance on the past, and you become free to enter the present. Revelatory experiences will then be continuous, and you will be restored to awareness of your original perfection. The emergence of formlessness and the explosion of inner light will then signature your entry into that still dimension of time; that is always **NOW**.

It is only because you exercise so little vigilance over the ego that you seem to have little to no control over the world of time. Both come and go, as one illusion. To your ego, times flows continuously from past to future and it ignores the present almost entirely. It has a visceral reaction to the present unless it serves some future purpose. Its endless scripts all-but guarantee that the lack of any real continuity to time is never known. So long as your world remains imaged through ego thought, you will believe, time to be both real and one-directional in nature. However, as I said before:-

"Past, present and future are not continuous unless you force continuity on them. You can perceive them as continuous and make them so for you. But do not be deceived, and then

believe that this is how it is. For to believe

reality is what you would have it be according

to your use for it *is* delusional."

[ACIM, T-13.VI.4:2-5]

(Sharon) Taming the ego is not easy. I cannot even tell when I am in ego mode, most of the time. It creeps in under the bed-sheets when I least suspect. **Do you have any practical method for slowing down time?**

(Jesus) There is a very useful technique for slowing down time practiced by advanced yogis for millennia. It can even be deployed to bring time to a complete standstill. They engage it to transport themselves into altered states of consciousness and to experience a far more fluid and boundless universe. Hence, they perceive through mystical vision the real essence of existence beyond all our filters. This technique is that of self-remembering. It is a simple technique to know but difficult to master.

Most cannot sustain self-awareness for very long. Within a minute or less, their consciousness will already be distracted and corrupted by external influences. Just about any random event crossing their inner or outer horizons is enough because they have not trained themselves to dis-empower all sources of distraction. Nevertheless reaching a supremely unruffled state of mental quiescence is a nec-essary pre-condition for entering the timeless and attain-ing to Yogic Samadhi. One just needs to cease all identifica-tion with the world of phenomenality and with all fluctua-tions of thought.

(Sharon) It sounds like this technique aims at block-ing out all sources of distraction. Wouldn't this also cause one to lose awareness of their immediate envi-ronment?

(Jesus) Not at all! One is to block out and inhibit nothing because this would demand energy, causing one to lose awareness. You are instead to remain non-identified and in a complete let-go! Your full release of all identifications is what enables you to effortlessly relax and yet be cogently aware of all that is happening around you. The arrow of your awareness will, therefore, be two-sided with one end focused outward on the world and the other focused in-wards on yourself, as the witness.

In contrast, identified awareness is one-sided because it just looks outward at the world. Thus hours or days can often go by before some unexpected event retriggers you back to self-awareness. Identified awareness is powerless to dilate time since it remains reactionary to events. Only increasing self-awareness has the power to dilate time. If you simply master this one technique, it can change the whole quality of your life. Your mastery of sports, music or any professional activity will also improve as a fringe benefit. The quality of your relationships will become elevated because you will always be authentically present and listening, and not on autopilot.

Your memory, focus, and recall will also be boosted, and your enjoyment of life will skyrocket. You will become expressly aware of the dream nature of existence. In fact, this one technique is a touchstone that can lead to your immediate awakening. In the meantime, you can use it to slow down the videotapes of your life and get some soulful R&R. Many use it to escape states of high anxiety, panic and fear and to climb out of ego mode. It lifts you out of the poisonous convoluted web of all your attachments and identifications and displaces you safely away from all that is happening.

(Sharon) From your description, it sounds like I have already run into this technique before. I heard it originally from reading the teachings of P.D. Ouspensky and had to give it a shot. So one night, while lying back in my recliner I began to practice it. I became very relaxed as I began to bring the light of my awareness back in on myself. Before long an entirely new quality had entered, and I had reached a supremely quiescent state of mind. I could see my body on the recliner. But now it seemed more like a dream body and was surrounded by a very pleasant energy field. Soon it became diffusive and lost all its boundaries to the recliner and the rest of the room. It began diffusing into endless space, and it felt like this space was also part of me.

Suddenly the entire living room seemed to come alive and was throbbing as one. All was vaporous including my state of consciousness, which felt boundless and untethered. Now, I was no "where" in particular. My body had become vibrant and amorphous and no longer restricted to any place or time. I was just operating as an unclouded serene presence hypnotically absorbed in the power of the present moment! There was this talk show going on TV. It felt like the host and interviewee were speaking directly into my ears or were they speaking out from them? — I could not tell! Their images now seemed to be in my living room as if the glass screen had disappeared. I felt, I could go inside the box and join them, any moment, or they could come out. All illusion of distance and separation had completely vanished. The sound from the TV began pervading the room embracing me in a total holophonic experience. Their speech was now so clear and slowed down, that I could reflect on every word, as it was being delivered.

Anywhere I placed my attention, there I was. I looked at my atomic clock. It was reading 8:44:24 pm. The seconds were going by, ever so slowly. After a short while, I started getting anxious and panicky to regain some physical bodily connection. Thus I got up from my recliner and started walking around but had lost all sensory connection to it. My body seemed more like an image in a dream or video game Avatar that I was piloting with a remote control. Part of the virtual reality in a tape called life. There was no one here but me. There had never been anyone here, but me.

At this point, every second had become so dilated that it seemed the second counter had completely stopped. I was actively goading it with my mind to proceed just one second more. I became terrified, thinking of what would happen if it completely froze and began cursing myself for ever practicing this technique. What had I done! I seemed to have unwittingly frozen time and could not get it going again. I became gripped with immense fear and anxiety. The videotape of my life was now at an almost complete standstill. I did not want to find out what would happen next. I was not ready for this!

Skywalker was sleeping on the couch nearby. It would be ten or fifteen minutes, at least before he awoke. That would be like lifetimes to me. I knew I would be stark raving mad by then and he would never know, what had gone wrong. I was living in an entirely different time-base to him, like I had fallen into a black hole and was looking out. Meanwhile, the same talk-show was going on and on. The voices had become so deep and slurred, like the random grunts of the incredible hulk. I tossed and turned in a feverish panic, yet did not know how to de-jinx myself.

Then an even more terrifying thought entered my head. *What if time started going backward?* It was scaring me to death. After all, I had already witlessly pushed the *pause* and *freeze-frame* buttons, so why not the *rewind*? The very fear that I would lose all sanity eventually rendered me unconscious.

When I awoke, the next day the videotape of my life was proceeding "normal," as before. However, now I was no longer fooled. I understood that time only ever rolls on at seeming speed it does, because of the limitations in our awareness. Sometimes we can tap into the mysterious dimensions and reach the spiritual awareness, in which this illusion melts away. Once our awareness becomes total, time will be frozen. The illusion of its continuity is due to our inherent dullness, firm dream identification, and powerful conditioning influences.

THE NONLOCAL UNIVERSE

(Jesus) Yes, many are very fearful of taking the lid of the jar. They think certain pieces of knowledge will burn and destroy them. So they cling tenaciously to very rigid notions of time and to a universe of separation. However, this picture is simply not true, and knowledge can only vaporize illusions. Such illusions derive from all those falsities one cherishes and reality distortions they aim to keep alive. As I said in the introduction to the Course.

"Nothing real can be threatened.

Nothing unreal exists

Herein lies the peace of God."

[ACIM, Introduction.2:2-4]

Even in the scientific world, the evidence is becoming harder to ignore. For example, in the field of quantum physics. Bell's theorem on quantum entanglement proves that our everyday perception of a "separated" universe, is clearly a mistaken one. Alain Aspect's experiments put it to the test and demonstrated that pairs of correlated photons could communicate instantaneously, even when supposedly separated by distances many light years apart. Nonlocal interaction is a known and confirmed fact. What this means to the layman, is distance is irrelevant when it comes to communication.

Of course, those visionaries, mystagogues, telepathists, channellers, and alchemists who have retained their connection with Spirit, already know this. However, scientists, materialists, skeptics and earthly types are usually the last to find things out because they are all doubting Thomases at heart. Then when they do find something novel, they jump up like an excited kid, who has just discovered the phenomenon of dry ice.

(Sharon) Isn't it possible that the photons are not communicating faster than light but are capable of instantaneous communication because they exist at the exact same place in a higher dimensional universe? So they are communicating instead through this higher dimensional construct, rather than the perceived universe?

(Jesus) You sound Irish alright. You quickly appeal to hidden variables and unseen dimensions rather than admit to the obvious explanation. The ego must love you and all those complex systems of mental calisthenics you craftily undertake, to divert attention away from the obvious. However, once again, what would Occam's Razor have to say about your opinion?

(Sharon) What is the obvious explanation?

(Jesus) That all spatial separations are illusory, and the particles have always been in the same place because they are in your mind. It is your mind alone that projects all illusions of distance in space. Nothing has ever been separate or apart from your mind and thought. Nevertheless, the higher dimensional construct does exist. It lies within and is far beyond that manifold of spacetime, you currently project.

(Sharon) Once again, it seems you are declaring this spacetime universe is a hallucination arising from our inner distortions — an appearance that has never existed as a fact? So long as we believe it is happening to us, we will continue to play the victim? We will, therefore, seek to avoid certain unpleasant aspects of our experience while amplifying others!

(Jesus) Exactly! The only useful purpose of spacetime is as a learning device that enables you to transcend it. Unless you use it as such, you will not heal. Thus you will remain blind to all the gifts, the present moment is endlessly offering to you. Function more like a kid with the keys to a new Maserati who cannot get his foot to the pedals. Once you discern the real purpose of your spacetime adventure, you will no longer seek to avoid any unpleasant aspects but welcome all that comes your way. You will drop all your defenses and come out of your shell and open up to each and every moment with tenderness, wonder, and awe. Then rapid progress will begin to occur because you will have finally taken responsibility for your self-made world.

(Sharon) Sounds easy! I should give it a try! I have nothing really to lose since my life is already in the dumps. I just had the epiphanic insight, that our concept of a nonlocal, non-separated universe could also help explain many of those parapsychological phenomena, for which there is a mass of emerging evidence!

(Jesus) Mind, has always been nonlocal because it is everywhere. In fact, it is more accurate to say that everywhere exists in it, because it has never existed spatially at all and space is but one of its derivatives. All those psychic abilities, such as remote viewing, clairvoyance, clairaudience, precognition, retrocognition, psychokinesis, etc. work because the mind is connected intimately with all its aspects. There is just One-Mind!

All the same, establishing a sound and reliable connection to this One-Mind can be difficult, if you allow the ego to rule the roost. The ego is like a jamming device that continuously interferes and drowns the Voice of wisdom out. It wants you to hear nothing, but its own crazy thoughts and endless rants about new devilish schemes.

(Sharon) So many experiments have now been conducted, on these parapsychological phenomena, that the evidence is becoming almost impossible to ignore. The profound influence, of our innate psychic abilities, has been proven statistically significant by anyone's golden standard. Measurement data extracted and crunched from a profusion of controlled experiments and double-blind studies have established outcomes that are hundreds of millions of times that of pure chance.

As a consequence, we now engage these abilities, as indispensable tools, in fields as diverse as investigative research, forecasting, crime solving, remote spying and espionage. Anyone can see, critical information is being tapped into, through underlying mechanisms that all classical theories or frameworks are powerless to explain. There is a chain of causality in place here; that will only be understood by transcending the limiting paradigms of our current world-model. It seems all information is available, if we just knew how to work it.

It is also becoming harder to discount all those mediums who have channeled revelatory information to us, in recent times. Some names pop into my mind including writers like Jane Roberts, Alice Bailey, Aleister Crowley, Helen Schucman, JZ Knight, to name but a few. Then there are psychic surgeons and healers like Edgar Cayce, Rasputin, and Zé Arigó, and artists that channel like Luiz Gasparetto, Valdelice Da Silva Dias Salum, and Nathaniel Bart. Obviously, some are more intuitively available to the wisdom and knowledge of the One-Mind. The rest of us seem to have very narrow filters, and toxic thought patterns cemented firmly into place. So generating so much noise as to blockade all psychic channels of communication. All of which becomes a critical obstacle limiting one's capacity to receive.

(Jesus) Yes, many are so preoccupied with small-minded thoughts and foolish obsessions, that it is almost impossible to reach them. You can see it for yourself in present day society. All those endlessly distracted by their cellphones or absorbed in their laptops. They do not understand that communication is a two-way affair. They are so focused on promoting their personal agendas or in marketing themselves, that they can no longer attune to the inner Voice of Wisdom.

THE MULTI-DIMENSIONAL UNIVERSE

(Sharon) Our current 3-D world model provides a totally inadequate framework for explaining psychical phenomena and other types of mysterious influence.

So there must be more evolved modes of experiencing our existence and possibly even worlds of higher dimensions?

(Jesus) There are higher modes of experiencing one's life and existence, and higher dimensional worlds. But these worlds of higher dimensions are not physical ones. Rather, they reflect fundamental changes in your inward evolution. In the 3-D world, you appear to live in; phenomenal processes are seen as the gods. They causally connect for you the worlds of form, function, movement and time. Without the information such appearances continuously convey to your senses, the world of your perception would appear so static, frozen and dead. You would feel blind.

Just reflect for a moment on a world without flat-screen TVs, i-phones, luxury automobiles, robots, rockets, drones and emerging nanotechnology devices and you would feel very joyless and lost indeed. Now take away your fast food, gaming technology, social networks, automation capabilities, etc. and the picture gets even worse. How about not being able to detect health problems, Tsunamis, earthquakes, changing weather conditions, ecological destruction, stock-crashes, etc. in advance? Great fear would soon emerge. You may end up regressing back to human and animal sacrifices in a foolish attempt to propitiate the gods of old gods.

Thus, all who experience the 3-D worldview have great respect for their modern day gods of gravity, relativity, motion, electromagnetism, electrochemistry, food chemistry, thermodynamics, radiology, quantum theory and so forth.

They see these gods, as saving their bacon some of the time and keeping them preoccupied and distracted for the remainder. The living experience would not be anywhere near what it currently is without these supernatural presences that produce all our toys and pleasure making devices. It is only natural that most will recoil very viscerally from anything new. Anything revolutionary to their current thought terrifies them. Nonetheless, when you start picturing some of these processes from a higher dimensional perspective, something truly remarkable begins to unfold.

Just take gravity, for example. From the 3D worldview, gravity is explained in terms of forces acting between fixed objects that direct their motions. Nonetheless, from the 4-D worldview, gravity is pictured simply as a frozen static curvature in the spacetime manifold. All has suddenly become quiet and inactive from the cosmological viewpoint. There is no more talk about objects moving about under the influence of mysterious forces. No more talk about a world of separation because all now are bum buddies, sharing the same blanket of curved spacetime. So, gravity becomes a very neutered dog, when viewed from a higher dimensional perspective.

This is not just true for gravity but also holds for all transient phenomena. Using the power of inductive reasoning and imagination, you can get a glimpse of how all active vibratory phenomena and vital processes can suddenly morph into something entirely frozen and static when seen from the higher operational manifold. Their transient aspect disappears either completely or in part, as you migrate up each dimensional layer. So very dynamic phenomena in the 3-D world flower into very static objects in the 4-D landscape and above.

As you progress to higher dimensions, more and more of the time aspect is stripped away, until eventually, no time element remains at all. So the illusion of time only arises from your holding an incomplete picture.

(Sharon) So is our 3-D worldview incorrect then?

(Jesus) No, it is not a mistaken picture, based on your current abilities! It is just limited and contextually bounded! Immersed and captivated by 3-D, you never see the truer reality. Instead, all comes to you extensively cloaked, laden with many unnecessary encumbrances designed to fool your senses.

In the 4-D worldview, nothing important changes or is taken away. The viewing context just expands to become a super-context of what you now know. You begin to see that the invisible gravitational force is just an apparition arising from a curvature of spacetime. So the 3-D view is a far less generalized, less potent understanding of the true nature of gravity. In the 3-D view, much is seen that is either unneeded or is not there. Your current concepts of planetary motions and forces are just like training wheels; that will eventually help you the grasp the higher view.

(Sharon) I am beginning to realize, that those who see through the eyes of higher-dimensional constructs, get a far superior picture. Their broader understanding empowers them to isolate and holistically capture true cause-and-effect relationships. Their capacities for mental abstraction and increased simplification bestows on them a new measure of power. Being able to generalize, they are no longer bogged down by the world of specifics. One could say, they have reached an increased evolutionary awareness and also a greater experience of timelessness.

(Jesus) Yes, the whole quality of their thought has changed in a fundamental way. Their very acute perspicuity enables them to lucidly reveal an image of the Absolute that is far more integrated and pure. The expansion of their thought abstraction capabilities reflects a quantum leap in their mental evolution. As one progresses upwards in the evolutionary chart, much that was perceived before disappears altogether.

When you attain a sufficiently high level of inner development, new dimensions start appearing in your perception. Simultaneously the world of objects, phenomena and spacetime begins to completely fade away. Spacetime is recognized now as just a constricting bodysuit. An unnecessary appendage arising from having a limited perspective and a lower order psychic-evolution. This clumsy artifact becomes completely engorged when one is immersed in the higher dimensional awareness. Eventually, one comes into contact with their true Self – the Faceless One. A pure effulgent Being that is wholly unified and forever changeless. One perfect, and infinitely potent. At this stage, all distortions and confusion imposed by lower order constructs is seen as totally superfluous.

YOUR UNDERSTANDING IS NOT ALWAYS NECESSARY

(Sharon) Many of those with psychic capabilities are just as clueless as anyone else, as to how they work? **Is an evolution in our understanding necessary to be able to use certain powers?**

(Jesus) Not at All! As I said in the Course, a full understanding of how to work miracles is not necessary to work them. In fact, you have already worked many miracles, most of which you do not even see! Your perspective is too limited.

> **"Miracles are habits, and should be involuntary. They should not be under conscious control. Consciously selected miracles can be misguided."**
>
> [Miracle Principal 5]

As with all higher powers, your understanding is not necessary to unconsciously employ them but it is necessary to gain mastery over them. From the perspective of higher dimensions, you already exist within these worlds, but this

higher image is lost to you because of all your mental filters and conscious limitations. For example, you can see
that a dog exists in 3-D, but the dog cannot see himself in
3-D. This is because the dog is incapable of thinking in concepts. The evolutionary capability of being able to use concepts and symbols is necessary to perceive in 3-D. You and
the dog also exist in 4-D, but neither of you can grasp this
picture. This is because you are still limited to thinking in
concepts.

However, supra-conceptual understanding is absolutely
necessary to perceive yourself in 4-D. Presently the 4th
dimension and its information come to you serially in the
form of time. Your evolutionary limitations impose penalties and results in your seeing a very fragmented picture.
Your erroneous beliefs, in turn, makes these fragmented
elements often seem contradictory. Even in the 3-D world,
You can see that dolphins and whales often communicate
using advanced multi-frequency sound modulation techniques, that we are yet powerless to decode. That does not
mean they have a clue what they are doing. They certainly
do not conceptually understand coding and modulation.
So, I wouldn't even bother asking them to highlight the
benefits of exploiting a Reed-Solomon algorithm. Likewise,
do you think every clown going around with a cell phone

or laptop could design one from scratch? Does this preclude a three-year-old from using such technological marvels?

All the time, you are harnessing the powers of a higher revelatory order without fully grasping what is going on. Nor do you fully comprehend the limitless causal potency of that Source, which sustains you. One that cradles your very existence and your every action. Many psychics have developed a higher intuition and are more tuned-in. Having eliminated the voice of nonsense and distraction, they can feel and intuit this supreme presence, even though it cannot be physically seen. They put this invisible intelligence to work for the good of all, by extracting critical information from it or using its powers to heal. All, without fully grasping the nature of the intelligence itself.

ARISTOTLE WOULD BE BAFFLED

(Sharon) To Aristotle, this world of our perception was all there was. To him, an objective world of 3-D appearances woven through time represented the very bounds of all existence. For a long time, afterward, we deceived ourselves into thinking this 3-D world picture is the entire truth.

(Jesus) Yes, and it made no difference how assiduously you consciously analyzed this space because this incomplete picture, itself, was always the problem. You had no way of deciphering that it was your poor evolutionary capabilities that imaged this world to you. It became fashioned out of all your shallow concepts, immense confusion, and often contradictory understandings. That is why it appears so split, fragmented, random and chaotic. For it represents a barren context in which effecting fundamental and progressive shifts can be very arduous to achieve.

(Sharon) It seems we are all in similar positions here and do not recognize the full extent of our ignorance. We function more like goldfish trying to understand the concept of an Einstein-Rosen bridge. Our symbols and concepts are powerless to point us to truth because they, themselves, are born from within this hopeless context.

We cannot perceive the 4-D world yet because our concepts hold us ransom. We need to transcend conceptual thinking altogether. Our experiences here are also false because they are made-up of images that are not there. The inner myths and demons we cherish produce a complete distortionary picture, which we then falsely identify with. It peoples our world with so many physically and psychologically crippled figures that we react to and call our lives.

(Jesus) All the same, you all have self-portraits engraved in the 4-D and 5-D landscapes, that you cannot yet see. That would require a psychic evolution in you that transcends conceptual thinking altogether. The current picture you hold, of bodies moseying about in a 3-D luniverse, is so comical in comparison. Even so, all tragic heroes in the dream hinge their entire identities to them.

(Sharon) So all the hookers, crooks and blow in our future, all our trails of tears and that despairing portrait of a body spiraling from youth to old age, is already statically imprinted in 4-D and 5-D landscapes, that we cannot yet see?

(Jesus) Yes, and it already exists complete within you! What unfolds into your conscious experience, only seems new. Moreover, all outer landscapes you perceive are intimately connected with all your mental movements, because thought and decision are part of its makeup and configuration. All landscapes you will ever know are outflows of your beliefs and inward evolutionary states. Nevertheless, what IS, is beyond all beliefs. As you make progressive changes, you will finally picture unalterable and immaculate Being.

GLIMPSING THE HIGHER DIMENSIONAL PICTURE THROUGH INDUCTION

(Sharon) I think it would fry my neural net if I were to perceive the 4-D world directly. I expect it would be far too much information to assimilate, all at once. Just as people who have been blind all their lives often can't handle or integrate the sensory bombardment when they are newly restored to vision. **I also wonder how the ego would survive in the 4-D world. Maybe it would become far more inventive or deceptive?**

(Jesus) The first step is to prepare yourself mentally for it. You can do this through the power of inductive reasoning and by comparing the changes involved in migrating from a 2-D to a 3-D world picture. Firstly, 3-D space is no different from 2-D space. It is the same space, just being interpreted differently. The perceptual content remains the same, yet the 3-D aspect only becomes revealed when you develop the capacity for conceptual thinking. Conceptualization functions like a magical decryption key, eliciting the 3-D picture into view.

Realize then, that it is highly-charged transformative changes within that unleash the extra dimension. Similarly, 4-D space is no different from 3-D space. Only when you succeed in seeing the world through new eyes and are capable of supra-conceptual perception, will it arise before you! Then you will be able to see the inside and outside of everything simultaneously and in all directions.

(Sharon) It just blows my mind. Imagine seeing the inside and outside of your lover's body all at once. All his or her organs, cells, sweat glands, blood vessels, layers of skin, etc. unfolded as a single picture. Just consider the impact this would have for surgery. A 4-D surgery procedure would be so advanced that tumors could be removed without every breaking or zapping through the surface of the skin. It would be neat for cosmologists too. They would be able to see the inside and outside of a black hole simultaneously and so grasp the truer picture of this unified megalith of energy.

I expect also that our problems with thievery and security would escalate substantially since a thief could now extract the contents of our safety deposit boxes without every needing to break the lock or seal. Then there would be all the privacy invasions and psychic intrusions. On checking in to our hotel, we could be able to see all the mischief and sex going on behind closed doors. So much for sleep!

The nature of our terrorist investigations would also be entirely transformed since we would be able to see all the trajectories of passengers arriving for their flight, to that fatal instant when their plane is blown up, as a single view. Our appreciation of life may improve since we would be able to see immediately, the entire life path of a person from birth to old age along with all the changes wrought in-between. Maybe we would develop more compassion, seeing the full enumeration of another's tragedies and joys, at once. It could be a very emotionally overwhelming affair.

I guess our concepts of life and death would radically change. Ego wars would become twisted into how much life-space each of us occupies in this higher dimension. Since we would know the exact instant of our death and of all those we care for, our decision making patterns would be utterly revolutionized. Also, seeing in advance, how our profession was going to be outsourced, to the lowest bidder in some third world shanty town, we may choose to embark on a very different career path.

(Jesus) Yes, I agree, most are not ready for this picture yet, and that is a big part of why they do not see it. There are many compelling and attractive advantages, but also some disadvantages. But Hey! If you want a simple life, crawl back into the 2-D world. Let me tell you that those who have experienced even a taste of the 4-D and higher realms could not ever consider going back and living in the 3-D one. I think they would be bored out of their minds within minutes. We all consider you folk flatlanders, since you are all hopelessly stuck in the mud of the lower dimensional spaces.

However one caveat, I will bring-up in advance and that is concerning depression. This can be even more insidious in higher dimensions. Because once you know for sure all the misery, up ahead, you may never want to get out of bed. The naïve happy bunny, that you are now will fast disappear once the ultimate futility of all you do, is clearly seen in advance.

For example, that company you are working so hard, for now, is going to lay you off, once they get their newest gaming system out the door. It does not matter that you are sacrificing your Christmas vacation for them or buying into their empty rhetoric about bonuses and promotions.

Since you do not know this yet, you go blissfully about content and unfazed. All pumped up like a Banty rooster, so proud of your accomplishments. Pussyfooting your way around the workplace, avoiding the undesirables ones and none of it will make a whit of a difference three months from now. Also, it can be humiliating to know the exact diapers one will be climbing back into in old age, even before they get free of their baby ones. Schizophrenia, paranoia, and other dissociative disorders can be particularly devastating experiential disorders to have beyond 3-D, as you can only imagine.

Fortunately, there are some great drugs for bombarding your neuroleptic transmitters in hyper-dimensional spaces. Ones that make current cutting edge SSRIs that only temporarily boost serotonin, dopamine and epinephrine seem like a cruel joke. These old world polypeptide transporters only alleviate anti-depressive symptoms at tremendous cost. Likewise for new drugs, like Intelleral that claim to increase sharpness and memory. They are like taking the snails' path through the axon airspaces via the synaptic call center. In the end, they all inflict enormous damage on your self-belief and detract from recognition of your own mind's power.

However, for those ready to up the stakes, the higher view also presents some incredible opportunities. You too can learn to adjust time and space for your maximum benefit. That is what I meant in the Course when I said:-

"You may think this implies that an enormous amount of time is necessary between readiness and mastery, but let me remind you that time and space are under my control."

[ACIM, T-2.VII.7:9]

In the end, it all depends on your attitude. You can decide to work those healing miracles which overcome all fear and be restored to love. Then this higher dimensional world is your oyster.

Also, the more elevated view will erase many misconceptions you currently hold, that are a consequence of your limited 3-D spatial perceptions. All that is illusory will be stripped away, and a truer understanding of cause-and-effect will be known. At present, you are continuously reversing these two and often failing to see them as one. This is a big part of what leads to your powerful state of confusion. In a way, you are no different from a 2-D being who perceives a static 3-D sphere as just an oscillating line.

Appearances do not make for reality, as you will soon find out. Many phenomena in your space, you cannot understand without gaining the higher dimensional view. Only the enlightened can correctly discern the changeless in the sea of change. They know, they have never really been born and will never die, despite all illusions to the contrary. Likewise, they comprehend that all seeming change arises from the distortions and limitations imposed by one's viewing lens.

Unfortunately, the evolutionary compulsion is to continue working on problems, which do not need fixing until one fully realizes there never was any problem. All your work and effort is necessary however to bring you to this realization. Your limited understanding is the problem. This is the soil in which all contradictions and perceptual distortions flourish.

Nothing new can ever actually happen because that would be declaring the world of time to be ongoing and still a work in progress. Nonetheless, there will be much that will seem new, as your understanding changes and increases. Your consciousness must evolve until you can finally glimpse the changeless. Eternity is always present, and you are Here! In fact, you Are the Kingdom of Heaven! What else could you be, since there is no separation? But without purification and evolution in your thought, you cannot know this. Your past, present, and future are one to God, who knows you only as timeless and perfect.

FREE WILL VS. DETERMINISM

(Sharon) There are certain aspects of all this, that I just don't get. In the Course, you never stop communicating about our great need of attunement to the Holy Spirit. You say His Voice can direct us, in making wise decisions. Now you are presenting a somewhat static final picture; one that seems somewhat independent of all our decisions.

(Jesus) Your decisions cannot change the final picture, but they can change your awareness of the picture. They are always just modifying the template, not the end result.

For example, there may be numerous paths up to the top of the mountain, but at the top, the view remains the same. You can use the power of your decision and free will to choose either a fast path or a slower one. On the more leisurely trail, you will not be changing much each day. You may not even go through any fundamental changes or evolutions of thought in a given lifetime. But one thing is for sure! You will need to go through all necessary evolutions required, to reach the summit. Forced to learn how to adapt to the crisp thin air that is at the top. The final height through which you will climb will also be the same!

What is on each path is already predetermined, because the mountain never changes. Your free will only extends to you the power to choose which path you will take. It does not change what is on each path. So you see there is no real contradiction between destiny and free will. Nor is there any such thing as having a fixed destiny, because you can always change your mind about which path you want to remain on. But unless your decision patterns change, your future is cast in stone. *'Alea Iacta Est'*, as Julius Caesar might put it. So which path will you choose? That trail which seems easier and more scenic at first? The one, in which you simply cave to your ego! Or will you choose the path that vastly accelerates your progress out of time? The very one that seems more demanding and arduous at the beginning?

When you attune to the Holy Spirit and follow His guidance, you are taking the fast path. He is asking you to forgive and this you can still find difficult. He is also asking that you be inclusive rather than exclusionary, to look out to fulfill the collective needs of all and not just your own selfish ones. So do you enter the high country of the mind, or procrastinate instead in the low country of the ego! Remember, His ultimate purpose is for your ultimate good.

Choosing the Atonement is deciding to practice quantum forgiveness. Thus you will arrive at the summit of Truth far sooner. This will help you circumvent many storm clouds along the way. Because, the slower routes, only seem easier in the beginning. In the end, your frustration and weariness increases on these paths and you encounter far more unnecessary pain and delay.

THE MISTAKEN PICTURE OF CAUSE-AND-EFFECT

(Sharon) You said earlier that real cause-and-effect relationships often become confused in lower dimensional spaces. Can you provide any examples of this?

(Jesus) Yes, there is a slew of bad things that can happen when one cannot see the complete picture. For example, these days you see on the news, stories of many prisoners being released from jail because of compelling new DNA evidence. All the same, they remained there for decades, often stewing on death row. Convicted, on the fragmentary evidence of a few biased witnesses or a piece of cloth. So it is also with many of the cause-and-effect relationships, that are identified, in the world of your perception.

A few of your misfortunate mistakes are **(1) Reversing cause-and-effect, (2) Not recognizing cause-and-effect circularities** and **(3) Being unable to discern when cause-and-effect are one.** So you often fail to see various phenomena as interlinked and just many different faces of the same beast.

Firstly perceiving yourself as in the world, is one example of a cause-and-effect reversal because the world is instead appearing out of you. Secondly, a classic case of cause-and-effect circularity is in the body's supposed circulatory system. The heart is perceived as the key agent responsible for pumping the blood around the body, which then keeps the brain alive. Then the brain's master control system, the autonomic nervous systems located in the hypothalamus, is supposed to be the center of intelligence or Bletchley Park, that keeps the heart functioning correctly and in all its right rhythms. So in this system, each effect seems to be a cause, and also cause of its own cause, which is clearly as anfractuous, as it is absurd.

For the third example, consider the case of a 2-D being walking around a line in its planar world. As he does so, he sees this line shrink to a dot and then grow back into a full-sized line. So he mistakenly imputes that the dot is the cause of the line and the line is the cause of the dot. He does not realize that this dot and line are really one and the same and that the only thing changing is his own viewing reference. It is his own movement that is causing all the apparent changes in his perceptions! Consequently, he experiences the line as vibratory, when it most certainly is not. The line possesses no inherent vibratory characteristics. Yet, experiencing it, the 2-D being would not doubt this experience and he would assume, it had some external cause.

So it is with all vibratory phenomena you experience in the 3-D world of your perception, including music, color, sensation, electromagnetic waves, cosmological events, etc. These vibratory phenomena seem everywhere, and yet you do not recognize how they are caused by psychological forces and understandings endogenous to yourself. These alone establish the baseline for your entire experience inside the matrix. All vibratory phenomena are the product of a moving reference, which is your thoughts and beliefs.

For example, dogs think moving vehicles are alive in much the same manner as people. That is why they bark at them. The dog cannot recognize the car as a static, inanimate object since it cannot see in 3-D. To it, the car is a changing field of percepts, just like humans. It reacts differently to us only because of its sense of smell, taste and its need for reward, etc. But it cannot distinguish any difference in the "*aliveness*" quality between its Master and a car. We are of the same order, in its world.

A dog pees on a tree, because it knows from its perceptual history that it can get away with it and that the tree is not going to follow it around and kick it in the rump. If a man's leg is still for a long enough time, the dog may infer it is a tree and go pee on it. We are all the same mysterious black boxes to a dog. It just reacts differently based on whether this particular sensory bundle is "conditionally" known to provide retaliation or reward. If cars dropped bones in its lap and rubbed it nicely on the back, it would begin to treat the car like its Master.

Similarly, just because of your limited viewing reference, you treat black holes and naked singularities as if they were somehow very different phenomena from the rest of the space you perceive. But they are just like the stalactites one sees in a cave. Except these particular ones shoot up and down, linking 3-D space to 4-D space and beyond. Often also they connect to higher spaces, invisible to you. You consider those sections of your 3-D space which do not run perpendicular to your view as a neutral vacuum, from a temporal perspective. That which does is interpreted instead in terms of mass, black holes, naked singularities, etc. All the same, all such phenomena can be seen as neutral vacuums from the vantage point of higher dimensional space.

THE SPIRIT WORLD AND HIGHER DIMENSIONS

(Sharon) You have mentioned angels surrounding us many times in the Course. I have listed just one instance below. Do angels, spirits and various unseen entities move and work through these higher evolutionary spaces?

"Around you angels hover lovingly, to keep away all darkened thoughts of sin, and keep the light where it has entered in."

[ACIM, T-26.IX.7:1]

(Jesus) Angels work effortlessly through all higher spaces because they are in contact with Truth and always in the light. Such hyper-dimensional portals are also no distance from you since they are all formed from the mind. The limitations of your conceptual understandings, however, prevent you from accessing them. So it seems to cast a veil over them, rendering them invisible. So the incredibly potent becomes lost to your awareness.

Angels freely enter any space where they are needed. Your emotional energy ripples across the Akashic field, drawing them into your presence. Their companionship, however, can only be felt through the inner eyes of your deepest intuition. So you are always surrounded by spirits, angels, and entities from those higher evolutionary spaces.

(Sharon) I grasp what you are saying. We are in the same situation in our relation to angels, as the bacteria and cells in our bodies are in relation to us. These bacteria and cells cannot see or know about us because we represent a life-force supremely above their own limited intelligence. Nevertheless, it is one that sustains them all the same. The nature of the relationship between ourselves and all those higher Beings and Spirits is similar to that between bacteria and us.

(Jesus) Yes, humanity tends to see all forms of intelligence as a mirror replica of its own. It even projects its very peculiar mode of intelligence and limited beliefs to God. So you think, that if you ever encounter space aliens, they will communicate through symbols, concepts, and forms and arrive in strange looking spaceships. Now this is all so childish!

Man's unique kind of intelligence, namely conceptual understanding is just one of millions of very diverse types of knowledge. Most forms of intelligence are mutually exclusive to our own. Aliens are present everywhere around us, right now, and yet you cannot see nor detect them because your particular form of intelligence is blind to theirs. Nevertheless, these alternate modes of intelligence can move quickly and freely through all the higher spaces and most don't need to go anywhere at all.

The aliens that man always fantasizes about have already arrived, and you do not know it yet. In fact, they have always been here. Only when your consciousness evolves beyond concepts, will you recognize their presence! They are continuously traversing across your perceived space this very moment. But, like the perfectly content flee on the back of a buffalo you remain supremely aware because you can conceive of no other existence, than yours.

CONSCIOUSNESS AND PERCEPTION

(Sharon) Can you provide another example of our mistakenly reversing cause-and-effect?

(Jesus) One far-reaching example is seen in the relationship most hold between the visible world and their consciousness. Each behaves as though they are born into this world, yet in truth, the world is born out of their conscious mind and thought. Consciousness alone gives rise to the world. It has no other source. This tacit understanding will lead to your Enlightenment. No one has ever been enlightened without first making this critical flip to their worldview.

Consciousness is spaceless. There is no inside or outside to it. It exists no *"where."* There has never been any real separation between what is idly thought by the mind and then seen in the world. No real separation between subject and object or between consciousness and perception. The illusionary belief that they are separate is because of the very distortionary delusions of split-mind. Split-mind fuels and propagates all illusions because it experiences its existence dualistically.

Subject and object are like poles of a magnet; that can never be found apart. Where there is no subject, no objects will appear! The relationship is equivalent to that existing between the reflections seen in a mirror and the one witnessing them. Where there is no creative observer, there can be no passive reflections. Such shadows are just representations in form, of that which is mentally thought. Even divine visions and holy perceptions still contain some degree of error because they are images and all images have boundaries and limits. When all error has been dispelled, nothing will be seen.

CONSCIOUSNESS AS THE REALM OF DUALITY

(Sharon) You said split-mind experiences its existence dualistically. Can you expand on this?

(Jesus) Firstly, you must understand that consciousness and split-mind are synonymous and both are the product of error. The original error was the TMI, which we spoke of before. This contaminated the mind so that it could no longer grasp Knowledge directly.

Consciousness can be said to be the realm of duality because a conscious experience is necessarily a dualistic one. Nevertheless, it can be engaged as an excellent tool to bring one into closer contact with Truth or else as a hindrance to distort and block awareness of it. The mind that knows with certainty will not be a conscious one because Knowledge precludes any uncertainty or false imprints of duality. In Knowledge, there is no separation between the knower and the known. All conscious experiences, on the other hand, always imply some degree of displacement.

Consciousness arose simultaneously with that strange notion of a personal "I" or ego. Until the ego is relinquished,
one remains plagued by dualistic beliefs. Consciousness
can be said to be the realm of error because it always contains uncertainties. It is incapable of Knowledge and only
appears when Knowledge is absent from one's awareness.
Its most Holy purpose is to help you dispel all ignorance,
temptations, and false identifications. Only then can you
take the quantum leap, in which you become subsumed by
Knowledge.

It is used most strategically, as a learning device, to lessen
and finally obliterate the ego. Thus you escape the mud of
the world. The star-studded end-goal for consciousness is
its own obviation. For example, suppose you notice a man
running frantically down the streets in an absolute panic,
claiming he cannot find his head. You shout back, "*Of
course you cannot locate your head because you have no
eyes with which to see it.*" However, he cannot hear you, because he also has no ears, with which to hear. What is one
to do? All you can do is put his head back on! Then all his
problems are solved. Then the question, "*Where is my
head?*" no longer arises.

Likewise, it is with you and your ego. Your ego has no head and therefore no purified inner senses for vision and hearing, by which to reach truth. It cannot heal its perpetual state of intense anxiety and confusion and is forever boiling over on the tiniest issues. Meanwhile, it goes around exuding airs of confidence and superiority which aim to conceal its absolute cluelessness about its identity. Behind the curtains, there is much sublimated hysteria and consternation, and that is why it is always prancing about asking so many meaningless questions. However, its questions are all born in the shallow barren soil of the relative existence, and this is the realm of all the headless ones.

Everywhere you go, you see all these lost ones pacing about frantically. It is impossible to explain to them that they are headless because they cannot hear, nor understand. They will distort and misinterpret everything you say, so no real messages can ever enter the hollow, superficial chambers of their coconuts. All you can do is to direct your consciousness wisely and so free yourself of your own ignorance. Only then can you help, to put their heads back on.

Simply remember then, that to be conscious is to be headless. Here is the piggybank of the ego, which it

loads to the brim with all its unnatural desires and fears. Here are all its treasures and every false belief you have considered worthy of endorsement. All covered in mold and lice, since the instant of the fall.

Thus does consciousness become a distorting prism and a block to true seeing and hearing! An enemy within turned against yourself. For it is but an instrument after all. The cruel and senseless world you now perceive is the end-product of all your distortions of consciousness. For this world has no existence and is merely a hallucination arising from your self-made distortions. That is why you witness to much nonsense, and mindless atrocities, and hear so many pointless questions — no hallucination ever is in a position to rightly advise. So like a budgie you keep banging your head against the bars of your cage, hoping this will serve as your miracle cure, for the blunt force trauma you continuously feel.

CONSCIOUSNESS, THE
PROJECTIONIST OF THE UNIVERSE

(Sharon) You have equated consciousness with a realm of error. Can you provide some more illumination on this?

(Jesus) Once the *I-concept* of the ego arose, you entered the illusory realm of split-mind. This is the dualistic realm of *Consciousness and Perception*. Consciousness is the active element of this duality pair and the power which projects the world. Perception is the passive aspect, and it functions as a mirror since it can only passively reflect the messages it is given. This world can never tell you what you Are! It can only ever image back to you, your thoughts and beliefs. Its very presence represents a mirage. One arising as a consequence of your loss of Knowledge.

Your only purpose here is to heal your mind of all wrong beliefs and thus transcend the false dualistic framework of *Consciousness — Perception*. Then this world disappears because it has never really been present. All is swallowed up in your return to Knowledge. Like any good mirror, perception images all your erroneous beliefs, so that you

can understand and correct them. The purpose of Atonement is to help you separate what you Are, from that
which you are not. You can never approach Truth directly.
Instead, you establish a reverse vector to it by expelling all
incorrect understandings. Then the Real World will arise
before you in all its eternal radiance and grandeur. All
phantasms and chiaroscuro born from your materialistic
and utilitarian conceptions will disappear from your mind.
Incorrect beliefs block your view and impede your natural
vision. Judiciously empowering reason to expunge all misunderstandings and misconceptions brings you to awareness of unity. Then you know your utter indestructibility
and infinite potential.

Consciousness is the realm of error because you are always employing it to conceive and perceive some external
thing or idea. Some sense of separation is always established between you and the unique object conceived or
perceived. In reality, there is no separation between the
seer and the seen. It is dualistic thinking alone which produces all notions of pseudo-separation. Befuddled and dis-
concerted by all its implicit errors and contradictions, your
distorted mind-frame projects what is then known as the
Relative Existence. Even so, consciousness is capable of
making progressive evolutions in its imaged content so as

to align them into close harmony with Truth. You can reach a superconscious state, so mentally pure, luminous, expansive and undifferentiated that all your ideations become light-filled and then the quantum leap to the Absolute can easily occur. In the meantime, the Absolute remains immanent and transcendent to consciousness. Consciousness is the tool that drives all learning progress and inward evolution, and it brings you closer to the Absolute. That is what I meant when I said:

"Consciousness is the state that induces action, though it does not inspire it." [ACIM, T-1.II.1:8]

The spiritual light of wisdom deep inside illuminates your perception while your conscious states drive all actions and movements. All progress derives from your intimate connection with Spirit. From the hidden paradise within, now lost to awareness emanate all experiences of Revelations. Only Spiritual light is creative in any real sense. Consciousness can never be creative because it is not whole, but distortional by nature. It, therefore, cannot generate light. As it evolves, you come closer to Knowledge. When the Relative Existence arose, Knowledge became substituted with the realm of duality.

Consciousness is a very influential medium for weeding out the false since it enables you to purify and expand your concepts. As you follow this process, you become capable of increased levels of mental abstraction and quickly eliminate all impediments interposed to the natural light of Spirit. The real work is in eradicating all your erroneous beliefs. Then meaningful transformation automatically occurs, and your perception becomes filled with light. All phenomena and motion appearing on the screen represent just passive reflections of your active states of consciousness. Changing your thoughts and beliefs is the way to heal and transform your world. Perception merely serves as a thought reflector; it is not a doer in any real sense.

If you expend your energy attempting to make progressive changes in the world without making any fundamental changes in yourself, nothing will ever be accomplished! All your comings and goings and that immense hive of activity surrounding you will be a complete waste of time. Just look at this world, as a blank slate, in which nothing is ever happening, and you will make excellent and rapid progress. That nothing is going on apart from your mental actions is the undiluted truth, that few speak! It is your thoughts and beliefs alone that produce all images and appearances you perceive. Dualities have no meaning in themselves. They always represent pseudo-splits in that which is whole, and they establish meaningless contexts, in which you become easily lost in dark passageways of thought. Meaning can only be restored by transcending the dualistic and thus healing the split in your mind. Nonetheless, dualities feel palpably real to anyone imprisoned in their false context, just as hallucinations can seem very real to the mind that generates them.

The overwhelming presence of illusions in your daily experience can make them feel so cogently real, that they are accepted as fact. The unreality of all dualistically based experiences becomes abundantly clear once you transcend all dualistic thinking. In each dualistic pair, you will notice that each half is meaningless on its own. For example, consciousness cannot survive without a world of perception, because it uses perception as the endpoint for its projections. Likewise, without consciousness, the mirror of perception, would serve no meaningful purpose. No half of a duality pair possesses an independent existence. Both halves can be considered split aspects in what is One.

Just as *consciousness-perception* are split aspects of Whole-Mind. Whole-Mind, being immaculately pure transcends both consciousness and perception. Only this Mind is capable of receiving and recognizing Knowledge. Consciousness and perception will remain learning devices that will ultimately disappear when no longer needed. They contain the essence of the Supreme Reality even though neither aspect can reach it directly. You will only reach to your original and transcendental state of mind when you have seen through the hide-and-seek game; your consciousness continually plays on you.

THE ABSOLUTE

(Sharon) How can we now when we have reached the Absolute?

(Jesus) When one looks and sees no more reflections, one has transcended subject/object duality. Then one has recaptured the unborn and found one's original face. Penetrated through to a luminous world devoid of all objects, contrasts, partitions, and differentiations. One that is self-sustaining and non-contingent on anything apart. Here there are no gaps or discontinuities, in which any illusions could interpose themselves. Here lies power forever unopposed. Here relative knowledge has come full circle and completely voided itself. For you have reached the non-symbolic and formless existence.

Here there is no concept, conceiver or conceiving. No percept, perceiver or perceiving. Conception and perception had merely attempted to package the Knowledge of Whole-Mind into false and limited constructs. Sought to bring the Absolute down into the container of consciousness. Even so, all they managed, to do, was to fashion a turbulent sea of false appearances. The potency and fluidity of the Absolute must become lost whenever we seek to cookie-cut it into our crude and worldly thought-forms.

The Absolute knows nothing of the world of form. If it did, it would be capable of erroneous understanding. Error and the world of form are synonymous and all the Relative Existence ever reflects. The Absolute cannot uphold the world of objects, phenomena or consciousness because these were all born out of error. When you remove all defilements and impurities from your mind, you will have reached back to Knowledge and the Absolute.

THE THREE STATES OF CONSCIOUSNESS

(Sharon) How can we tell if we are making progressive changes in our level of Consciousness?

(Jesus) There is an evolution of consciousness which may be considered an evolution in your awareness of true Being. Not that being has any levels or partitions, but it can seem to be so endowed when experienced through the limited prism of consciousness.

The three levels or states of consciousness are that of solid, liquid and gas. Solid represents the strict, controlling and decimating consciousness of the tyrannical ego self. This type of consciousness is only capable of projecting a static world of objects. It presents a world where all phenomena are rigorously defined by their fixed functions and attributes. Everything is valued here only from a utilitarian and exploitive perspective. This is known as '*identified consciousness*' because it perceives itself as inhabiting a body and embedded in a world of form. Nevertheless, it feels threatened by everything that moves or breathes in the bleak world it sees. So it meticulously builds up a vast defensive network around itself. It is the furthest from Knowledge in the existential sense and also the supremely unhappiest.

Next up, is the liquid state of consciousness. This is the *logos-mind*. In Zen, this is the evolutionary state, in which an experienced meditator has so acutely questioned the world of her perceptions that she has come to the sagacious realization that "*The Mountains are no longer Mountains.*" This stage of consciousness is a necessary precursor to Enlightenment. One is now actively opening up and allowing the static boundaries between the inner and outer spaces to flow and smoothly interact. That fixed notion of a tyrannical ego self, has all but disappeared. It presents a world of superfluidity, in which the outer world is starting to melt and move about like water. All seeming external objects lose all their rigidity, sharpness, and very defined attributes. Meanwhile, the inner world is undergoing seismic shifts and volcanic eruptions of healing transformation. So the outer is just reflecting the revolutionary progressions happening within.

The liquid state of consciousness is however also a time of great turmoil because one is uprooting all false knowledge and mental conditionings, doggedly implanted since time began. There is a new glimmer of hope and a pervasive intuition of something absolutely new and transcendental about to emerge. All notions of victimhood have long dissolved — these were always the flipside of the tyrannical ego's control booth and the cost of giving it precedence in the mind.

Now the real relationship between inner and outer is becoming known, and one no longer pretends to be a victim. Nor does one see themselves as some mere object in an alien luniverse. You are beginning to capture at last the world' entire dependency on your state of mind. Grasping how adapting and uprooting your existing thought patterns transforms your whole world experience. So all is starting to flow, and all boundaries are disappearing. Form is moving into form and space is gobbling up space.

Finally, one enters the gaseous or vaporous state of consciousness. Here Spirit and Atman are revealed. This vaporous state is always coincident with an explosion of the inner light of spirit outward into the world of one's perceptions. No objects or phenomena have ever been able to withstand the power of this light. It heralds from the eternal and the formless into the world of spacetime and form. The emergence of formlessness is coincident with the dis-

appearance of all that is phantasmagoric and unreal. Everything disappears, and one's true Self is known. One realizes now both viscerally and existentially that the world of
perception and all accumulated memories were part of a
show going on in a hallucinatory and empty universe. A
dramatization of ego scripts which functioned to establish
false overlays over your mind. Vicious imprints stamped
into perception, that all-but-guaranteed you would not see.
But now you have reached the zero point of consciousness.
What can be called the *consciousness of consciousness!*
Now, since consciousness has taken itself to be its own object of investigation, it has stopped projecting form. In this
unique state of contact with true Being, one has transcended all dualities and can work miracles of healing with ease.
Revelations is an everpresent experience. One has come so
close to the Knowledge of Spirit, that the Relative Existence completely disappears. So you begin to see yourself
flickering in-and-out of existence, like an apparition in a
dream.

First there comes the feeling of "**I Am**," followed almost
immediately by "**I Am Not**." These oscillations signature
your accession to the root of all Being and the source of all
projection. The feeling of "**I Am**" occurs whenever you are
identifying once again with your streams of mental projec-

tion. Then the screen of the world arises back into your awareness. For the tiniest fraction of time, the world seems to be! Then comes the recognition "**I Am Not.**" This blankets and suffuses your awareness so profusely that it dawns on you, that you are the projectionist of all dreams. Now seeing through the vision of Spirit, you perceive nothing at the level of form.

This feeling "**I Am Not,**" is the essential backdrop of all existence — the indestructible plenum of the unmanifest which potentiates all manifestation. The manifest, in contrast, is that which tricks you into believing you are a phenomenal being. But now you have come to know your Noumenal and Eternal Face. You are presented with an avalanche of pure information. Arrived at that ever-existing fullness that is also a nothingness. This vaporous state of consciousness is one of deep bliss and relaxation because you are immersed in a vibrant sea of formlessness and present at the hub of all Being. You now have complete mastery over the phenomenal universe and bask in your one True Home!

THE POWER OF CONDITIONING

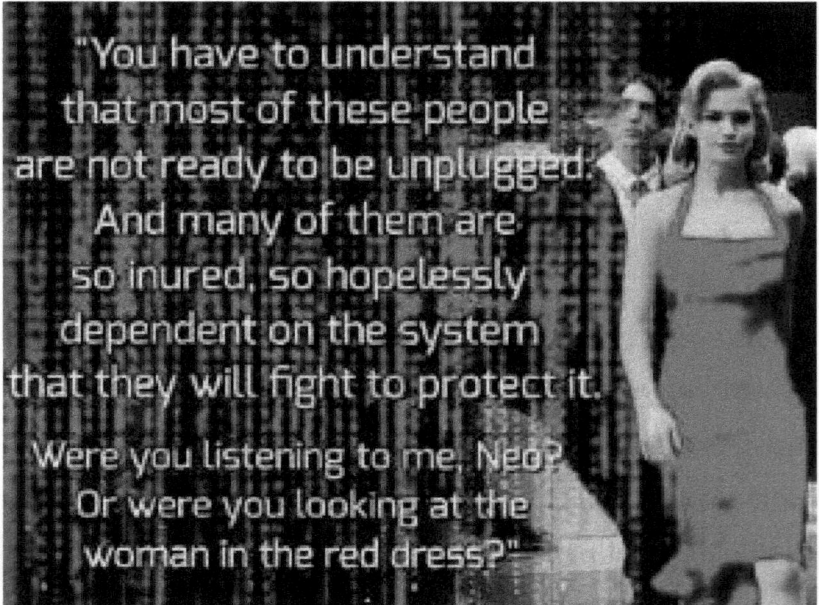

"You have to understand that most of these people are not ready to be unplugged. And many of them are so inured, so hopelessly dependent on the system that they will fight to protect it. Were you listening to me, Neo? Or were you looking at the woman in the red dress?"

(Sharon) You have spoken many times on the power of conditioning. Taught how it blocks the real from our experience while keeping us at ransom to less evolved states of consciousness. **I would like to learn more on this!**

(Jesus) At any given level of consciousness, you witness only those life-forms that seem trapped and bound in lower states of conscious evolution. You never witness those above your own! You may intuitively feel or even inductively grasp that there are progressive developments in consciousness, above your own. However, you can only truly know them by becoming the higher evolution they represent.

It is just like you are in a skyscraper looking down at all the buildings and people below. Seeing them scurrying about like ants, exhibiting all the neurotoxic bombardment of the information age. All their actions and behavioral patterns are so pre-programmed, superficial and predictable to you. They all function like the quaint little toys, they are designed and conditioned to be. For a moment, you exude a central air of superiority and contempt and feel yourself to be king of the castle. You are anything but!

Now take a dog, for example. It can only experience the world of people, as filtered through its own limitations and unique knowledge-base. In a way, it must experience all mammals as possessing qualities very similar to its own. It can know nothing of our dreams, hopes, anxieties and frustrations. Nothing of the wicked pleasures we seek and of the various mental illnesses that plague us. If it were to get a glimpse into the inner world of our thoughts, even for a moment, it would have nothing more to do with us. All the joy would fast disappear out of its bark, once it fully real-

ized, it was paying homage, all this time, to the clearly insane. All those freaks, vagabonds and bona fide misfits that
are seen roaming about everywhere on psycho-planet.
Fortunately for the dog, all such ideations get filtered out,
so that it can go its own merry way. In this sense, ignorance can be bliss.

Likewise, when we peer down into the murky well of our
bodies we see all those microscopic cells, bacteria, lice, and
tiny little organisms crawling about in it. All blissfully unaware of the toxic dumping grounds in which they live.
Their lack of comprehension and evolutionary capacities in
this is their saving grace. As it is for all those computer vi-
ruses, we bit-blitz into our computer chips and across our
cyber-tunnels of destruction. The filter of conditioning can
be a sound protection device until one is ready. That is
why 99.9% of humanity eagerly swallow up the blue pill.

I said before that *perception is learning.* So the world you
see is continuously tracking your states if consciousness
and picturing them back to you. This is the key mechanism
that enables your learning to progress and your consciousness to flourish. Consciousness can, therefore, be
viewed as an ever-expansive array of ever-evolving psy-
chic-constructs. The extent of your evolution, in turn, de-

termines the multi-dimensional depth and quality of the world you perceive. Constructs that possess increasing flexibility, potency and scope enable you to evolve rapidly to a higher dimensional view. Likewise, they can transport you expeditiously out of the world of time.

The natural light of spirit is that which illuminates this array in your mind. However, this pure spiritual light is filtered, refracted and distorted as it passes through the maze, by your inherent ignorance. Collectively this includes all your limitations of consciousness, judgments, conflicted beliefs, and unworthy aspirations. It also includes all your biases, prejudices and general state of closed-mindedness. In the end, so much light is lost or blocked, that little remains to illuminate your true perceptions.

Your twisted mind can rapidly turn Heaven into Hell. This matrix of ignorance can be thought of, as the ego. It drives all your beliefs in separation and change. The ego itself is a myth that can only maintain its lies through bribery and your complicit self-deception. The Atonement has the purpose of undoing this vast edifice of falseness. Thus it empowers you to enter the transcendent realm of the present. When you reach to the Knowledge and Wisdom the Absolute, it will be abundantly evident, that your core Self, has always existed peacefully in an eternal sky.

THE EVOLUTION OF CONSCIOUSNESS

(Sharon) How can we recognize when we are ready for an evolution in consciousness?

(Jesus) The first signs are increasing disenchantment and even despair. Once you are no longer satisfied with your existence, at a very fundamental level and no longer tempted by the superficial gifts of the ego, you are ready!

For example, we said before that a dog only understands the higher reality of man, as filtered through its own limitations. While it is happy being a dog, it will not evolve any higher. It will only progress when it loses all interest in remaining a dog. Once it starts to feel its life to be incredibly tiresome, repetitive and utterly mundane, something tremendous is possible at last. Its chronic state of disillusionment establishes the necessary space within it for an upward evolutionary thrust to happen. Until that moment, genuine progress just remains potential.

(Sharon) So you are saying the dog must begin to hate its life entirely. See it as a dog's life and dread going through another doggy day of eating nothing but dog food. Maybe then, it would become like a Zen dog and start questioning the wisdom of barking at people and smelling other dogs. It would unquestionably begin to stick out sorely and seem like a real oddball in the world of dogs. The dog psychiatrist would be worthless to cure him or to restore the vigor in his bark. He may label him a borderline dog with depressive tendencies or delusions of grandeur.

(Jesus) Psychologically, he would no longer be a dog, and yet he would still seem like a dog to other dogs. He would smell the same, look the same and still quack like a duck, as they say. He would no longer occupy top-dead-center on the Bell-curve of dogs but would be a fringe outlier instead. All the same, other dogs would quickly dismiss all these nutty idiosyncrasies, weirdness, and spiritless barks. His behavior though peculiar, would not be taken too seriously.

(Sharon) I gather your analogy goes deeper than just describing a chance encounter with the Socrates of dogs! I expect this dog's tale is just a precursor to man's and what we must go through if we are to evolve to the supra-conceptual realm.

(Jesus) Yes, all around you, within and without lies the transcendent realm of the unmanifest. This provides the existential basis for all that is seen and unseen. Even though you cannot see, touch, hear or smell this realm with your current level of conscious evolution, all appearances you perceive are fashioned out of it and depend on its power. All becomes perfectly imaged to correspond with your current conscious abilities. All objects and perceptions just witness your own internal filters and capacities.

Your handicap is your own. This alone prevents you from voyaging beyond the pale. A more evolved consciousness cannot reveal itself through lower order constructs. These constructs become containers that limit it, far too excessively. You have implemented so many containers that prevent revelations and these include all those concepts, symbols, percepts you employ, to better understand yourself. All the same, the Supreme One must remain transcendent to all such containers.

Cosmic consciousness does not need to do its jig through limited frames and contexts. All orders, levels, and partitions arise out of that suffocating mental cloud of your personal limitations. A higher order consciousness when progressively restricted to lower order constructs may appear as a man, a dog or a rock, etc. This man, dog, and rock are just like pictures or vignettes of the higher order consciousness viewed from progressively smaller frames.

Thus consciousness may become imaged in high definition 4k video, together with surround sound or else in low-quality black-and-white. All depends on the evolutionary capacities through whom it is emerging. So the spectrum of consciousness is just the spectrum of all limiting containers that we artificially impose over the higher order manifold. As your consciousness evolves, the dimensionality or your world will increase, as will the abstractive capabilities and potency of all the forms you will see. The real world remains unhindered by all limitations imposed by your poor spiritual vision and lack of conscious evolution.

Although the Absolute interposes no limiting artifices before itself, all modes of consciousness operating below perfect Knowledge will be unstable and in constant flux. So accounts for all your fleeting perceptions and the world of time.

HOW LIMITING CONSTRUCTS ERASE MEANING

(Sharon) You have spoken about how limiting constructs can reduce our understanding. I would appreciate it if you could provide some examples.

(Jesus) To better understand this, let's invite back our friends from the 2-D realm. They will illuminate how a limiting context can cause one to lose access to meaning,

For example, suppose you place a circle on the 2-D landscape and ask a 2-D being to explain this phenomenon, how will he respond? Because of the limiting constraints of his 2-D world, he can only perceive a circle as a line. However, unlike other lines in his space that oscillate in size as he walks around them, this one has a unique quality that it can preserve its size.

The circle will just appear as a line and retain this peculiar extra property of being able to preserve its size, independent of his motion — sound familiar? It would be as light to us, a phenomenon that always retains the same velocity independent of our motion relative to it.

Our 2-D friend will have to take the phenomenon of a circle, exactly as it presents itself to his senses. He will be unable to distinguish it much from other lines, despite the fact that is completely different. He does not have access to the higher dimensions that could explain its mysteries to him. Instead, he will somehow credit his mysterious walk as preserving its queer qualities. He will not understand that appearances, which seem the same, can yet be vastly different. He will attribute this particular line's weirdness more to his walk, than to some property intrinsic to itself. So its actual reality becomes masked by the limitations of his world. He thinks his picture of the universe is meaningful, but in fact, it is meaningless.

If I place a dot in the center of this circle, he will never see it. He will, therefore, assume this dot, does not exist. So if our 2-D friend takes existence as limited entirely to the field of his direct perceptions — he will miss out on a large chunk of the picture. Likewise, you assume those unseen universes lying outside your own capacities for spatial perception, do not exist. Nor could the 2-D being, ever comprehend how we could place a dot in the center of a circle, without first breaking its surface. Just as you cannot fathom the extraction of someone's inner organs, without first breaking the surface of their skin.

Similarly, if we ask our 2-D friend to describe a cube, he will be totally clueless. The 2-D landscape where it lives isn't a meaningful enough framework to provide any answer. This limited context needs to be transcended, for the answer to be known. For this, the 2-D being must undergo a fundamental inner shift in his Identity. One in which his mind evolves so that he becomes capable of 3-D projection. When this change happens, his self-image disappears as a 2-D being and he reemerges as a 3-D one.

Likewise, once a new evolution catalyzes in your consciousness, you will be able to project an entirely new world model. One that far surpasses all the limited meanings, inherent in your current 3-D construct. This new paradigm will be backward compatible with the 3-D world you now perceive, but it will be far more revolutionary and persuasive in its depiction. You will be able to see exactly how spacetime is bent and shaped and where whole sections are bypassed entirely. You will be able to go through the paper of the spacetime manifold instead of having to experience it serially. Thus instantaneously arriving at portions of it that now seem far-distant in your future or far back in your past. Yes, you will be sliding down Einstein-Rosen bridges inside your mind, like you are on the slide on Waterworld.

The Course guides you on your journey to formlessness and to perfect understanding. Along the way, your thought abstraction capabilities will be greatly enhanced.

THE VECTOR OF BEING

(Sharon) I am beginning to understand now, how a limited context can cause lost access to meaning. By denying us the fuller picture, it can often lead to confusion as well as false interpretations of true *cause-and-effect.*

I also believe, the limitation of our current worldly context is a substantive part of the reason we grow old, weary and die. After a while, nothing seems to stimulate us here any longer. We begin to see our newest experiences as just more variations on old themes. We soon realize that we are not growing substantively with the years. Our understanding has become static and dead and has not changed in any fundamental way in decades. There is nothing cogently fresh and vibrant happening within us, as there was when we were young.

(Jesus) Many wise and matures souls have come to this realization. For example, the mystic G.I. Gurdjieff understood this intimately, as did his protégé P.D. Ouspensky.

Gurdjieff passionately taught that we are always simultaneously maturing in two completely different and seemingly irreconcilable directions. He termed these **(1) The dimension of our knowledge** and **(2) The dimension of our being.**

When we are evolving along the dimension of knowledge, we are gathering more-and-more exoteric and esoteric facts about the world around us. That is accumulating more information, memories, perceptions, insights and also identifying more cause-and-effect relationships that help explain the various phenomena we perceive. This strategy, however, must eventually lead to the point of diminishing returns. One in which, we are making no further pivotal progress in our worldly understanding and exact relationship to it.

It is not long before we reach an unavoidable bottleneck, after which we feel ourselves existentially forced into being mere stamp collectors of our world. One could even say; we become relegated into the garbage collectors of this landfill. Despite our astronomical collection of tons more data, there are no far-reaching and capacious evolutionary shifts happening within.

Instead, regardless of all our ingenious interpretations and endless number-crunching, we are extracting no more meaning from it all. Even our ever-developing portfolio of life experiences seems powerless to help because our lives are increasingly becoming very flat, empty and circumvented. We are getting about the same high as an alcoholic after decades on the booze. We can hardly tolerate going through the motions of this humdrum existence another day and begin to dread the immense boredom that lies up ahead.

Many, for instance, are extremely erudite in worldly knowledge and capable of significantly accelerated learning potential. Often also, they possess eidetic memories and are very quick and flexible in dealing with various higher concepts and mental operations. But something inside them is dead. These are the rain-mans, prodigies, idiot-savants and high caliber intellectuals of our world. They have progressed very extensively along the dimension of external knowledge and yet their beings remain ravaged and highly undeveloped.

Often they cannot even drive a car, or cook for themselves. So they stay indoors, most of the time nursing a host of very odd and diverse phobias. No one will go near them anymore because their unique combination of rare and eclectic idiosyncrasies turn one off. In many cases, their knowledge has become so twisted and perverted, that it renders them incapable of functioning productively at all.

One thinks of figures like William James Sidis, Alexander Luria, and John Nash. William James Sidis was a childhood prodigy with exceptional mathematical abilities and learning capabilities, but he spent most of his vintage years collecting train timetables. Alexander Luria had an eidetic memory but was at a total loss when making rudimentary value judgments. John Nash was the famed mathematician who won the Nobel Prize in economics. Nevertheless, he was delusional and suffered from schizophrenia and therefore found it difficult to function smoothly in society. Nor could he ever develop strong interpersonal relationships.

Likewise, we are aware of a host of luminary figures such as Hui-Neng, Lao-Tzu, Bodhidharma, Atisha, Ramakrishna, Sri Ramana Maharshi, Osho and numerous others who they have penetrated profoundly to the very depths of Being and reached Self-Realization. They were all naturally endowed with a higher mystical intuition and capable of reaching very elevated states of spiritual understanding.

Even though their worldly accomplishments are often minimal and vocabulary no greater than a high school student, they had a highly contagious and influential impact, on all they met. They exemplified the power of pure Being in motion. Having uncovered in themselves, the primordial Self-resplendent One, they provided direct insights into its wisdom and had an active and lasting impact.

There often rolls in a crisis point in our lives. One in which, we have progressed to the peaks of worldly knowledge but cannot reach any higher unless we undergo a fundamental evolutionary shift, at the level of our Being. We can easily conceive, for example, how a 2-D being, who has become an expert in all worldly phenomena must eventually feel very bound and trapped by this limited context. He will begin to see it as his prison-house and may become severely depressed. Only an evolutionary change at the level of his being can bring him out of this depression. Just seeing more lusterless appearances in his world, isn't going to do the trick.

To effect this evolution, he must begin to focus the arrow of his awareness on the fundamental basis of all his knowledge and reevaluate all his perceptions, in a compellingly new way. He must come to see all limitations of his world, as arising from within himself. Recognize that this endless flood of appearances, is not Reality but simply a mirage reflecting his handicaps. Doing so, he will know, that what appears the same can be so very different and yet what seems so different can yet share the same essence. Only then will he have that seismic life-changing epiphany, in which his inner light explodes out into the world of his perceptions — thus illuminating it in an entire new paradigm-shifting way. Only then, can he take the quantum leap in his consciousness and emerge as a new being capable of 3-D perception.

WHAT AM I ?

(Sharon) In the Course, you emphasize the question **"What Am I?"** as the panacea to escape all conflict. Can you provide some insight into its importance?

"There is no conflict that does not entail the single, simple question, "What am I?" "

[ACIM, WB.139.1:6]

(Jesus) All dreamers hinge their existence on a vast array of untruths. Fallacies, they then become too frightened to expose. Denial and self-deception are very powerful forces that keep all illusions alive in the Relative World.

The ego mind likes to cling and demands full control. This is one of its primal survival mechanisms. So it grasps tenaciously to the dark maze of all worldly attachments and works incessantly compiling a list of all that makes it feel important. This catalog includes all its supposed friends, its experiences, credentials, virtues, and abilities. It even gets attached to its life story, its evil schemes, infamous pursuits and all its "sacred" judgments.

It leverages all such foolishness to increase its self-worth and specialness in the eyes of others. It fully believes this haze of the illusory offers it protection against a fearsome capricious world that shows no mercy. It is terrified of the void of self-annihilation and believes, were it dispossessed of all this nonsense, it would rapidly fall from grace and perish. All these idols do is establish rigid barriers between ourselves and others and to life in general. They make it impossible for one to be spontaneous, adaptable and authentic.

The question, **What Am I**? in contrast, serves as a very powerful means to rid yourself, of all self-deceptions. It is the spiritual cure for quickly dispelling all false knowledge. So it functions as a very potent charm, to elicit the truth of what you Are. It expunges all ignorant notions you have gathered throughout time. An added bonus is that it works very efficaciously to disempower the ego. It represents a silent appeal to your mind to find an answer at a level deeper than the question itself. By migrating your consciousness into the personal and subjective dimension and beyond the world of mere externals, it can bring you genuine and pure understanding almost immediately. As soon as the light of the projectionist is turned back on itself, all false identifications that surround the mind begin to clear away.

Once you begin to faithfully apply, this introspective technique indiscriminately to all aspects of your life, something truly beautiful and freeing starts to transpire. You begin to realize its tremendous healing capability. You were unnecessarily holding on to too much junk, thinking these trinkets were your only source of salvation. Now you see that you are not your possessions, accomplishments or titles. Not even your body, gender, social status or life experiences. Nor anything you see, hear, smell, touch, or think. Instead, you are the source of all sensation and the silent witness of all thought.

So this question brings you the raw core of your subjective experiencing and dispels all ego myths. Your real Self cannot be fashioned and molded into any object of knowledge. It is beyond all objectivization and conception. The conceiving mind can never be any object it conceives. Just as a mirror is not any image it reflects. You likewise are that miraculous indestructible awareness in which all worlds appear. The enormous fringe benefit of this question is that it silently swallows up the ego. Because the ego is always seeking to have you identify, not just with your possessions, but also with your beliefs, feelings, convictions and inner experiences. Now, for the first time, you learn how to disidentify and remain non-attached. So you are placed on the royal route to freedom.

Soon you find yourself penetrating fearlessly into the subjective realm, that you had been ignoring for far too long. The ego, in stark contrast, likes to live predominantly in the objective realm while actively dismissing the subjective realm altogether. It craves all those silly questions you incessantly raise concerning unexplained phenomena, worldly mysteries, celebrity gossip, alien lifeforms, etc. Even so, for every answer, you provide it with, it will ask a thousand more. The objective existence is its haven of safety and one that seems to guarantee its permanent presence in your mind.

What it will not tell you, is that all objects, phenomena, idols and temptations you perceive are just apparitions appearing out of your split-mind. They arise of nothing but your judgments, imaginations, incorrect understandings and wild projections. Even so, one who chases such superficial things is unlikely to know this. All its questioning and

explorations are meaningless because it is forever charter-
ing a course deeper into the non-existent. The ego, therefore, sets you on a fruitless path and one that can provide
no access to meaning. Since the "outer" world is merely a
mirage, it is incapable of pointing you to any watering hole
that can quench your real thirst. The only meaningful
questions you can ask are ones that interrogate it at its
very foundations. Only in such manner, can you expose
this false dualistic framework in which the ego has you ensnared.

The question **"What AM I?"** puts an end to all this futile
chasing after your own shadow. It functions to bring you
into the projecting booth, where you can be instantly lib-
erated from all that nonsense, you cling to out of fear. Both
aspects of your dualistic existence are allowed to come together and merge. So does your real relationship to the
world become apparent! This then terminates all meaningless ego questions forever. You lucidly capture how you
were duped for countless lives. Consumed by so many new
theories and inventions; that pertained to the world *out-
there*. Set on a futile journey, searching for meaningful
causal connections, where none could ever be found.

All your physical and mental energy was being wasted on quixotic pursuits. Meaning was never separate from your mind. However, this could never be grasped because of the dark covering you had interposed. The ego masked all meaning from your awareness. Born in the soil of your ignorance, it perpetuated an abode of hopelessness where nothing but contradictions reigned. All the savagery, mindlessness, and chaos you experienced reflected a cold and cheerless landscape which the ego shaped in likeness to itself. One in which it alone seemed to rule.

The question **What Am I?** Brings hope at last because it is asking you to change. Not at the level of Truth, but only at the level of illusion! The outer world has never been the problem, but you denied your role as its cause. Thus you forgot yourself as its dreamer and became caught up in its twisted paths. Now your focus is shifted to where real progress can be implemented. Over time, you cease to ask meaningless and trivial questions. Your mind becomes increasingly divested of all false concepts, illusions, and worldly knowledge. All that which functioned as an impediment to your Self-Realization. You begin to see through all the tricks in the ego's bag; all that which served to reinforce your false notions of duality.

SALVATION

(Sharon) You have expounded very competently how to expose all those personal myths, delusions, and self-deceptions that keep us far from Truth. It is evident, we all leverage a multiplicity of euphemisms and various forms of denial as a buffer against naked and raw disclosure. We feel that a bare bones encounter with unadulterated Truth would hurt or destroy us. We, therefore, keep it carefully concealed in a dark hazy fog and barred from all conscious awareness.

A more honest appraisal would proclaim that we prefer anything but the truth. Because it is evident, our ego trembles whenever the truth is near. However, it seems there is still another dimension to our problems. Our failure to make spiritual breakthroughs has a lot to do with our inertia and negativity. Our minds are so full of grievances and toxic thoughts that we go about incapacitated, self-crippled, and closed-off most of the time. In a private war with life.

You have stated before that our grievance-laden minds are a primary barrier to our Salvation. Can you now provide more detail on this?

(Jesus) Salvation can only be found by diving deep within and uncovering the unconditional love in which you were created. Truth is not fearful. It can only heal, and this automatically brings you to light, strength, peace, and joy. However, there is a dark cloud that surrounds your mind that most are too fearful to enter. This dark cloud stands between where you live most of your life and the naked truth. This cloud has developed since the beginning of time and is composed of all your grievances, mistaken beliefs, traumas and past failures. This dark cloud is all that separates you from your real Identity. It is the natural outcome of living in a body and investing in the ego. In this cloud, there is nothing that is real, but much that you are yet persuaded by.

Choosing the ego and its miscreative thought guarantees this dark covering will remain over your mind. Grievances are the inevitable outcome of feeling trapped within its thought. So long as you appear to be in the world, there will always be justification for grievances. The grievances of various health and financial problems, broken relationships or of not being fully appreciated. Grievances are the natural consequence of having a stake in the world and seeing the source of salvation as outside. Sadly, the universe, being ultimately unreal, must always disappoint. It has no treasures, no lasting relationships, and no abiding joys. It can provide no enduring platform of stability on which to hinge your sanity. There is no way for a mirage of your mind to satisfy your thirst. This realization must lead first to disenchantment, then resentment and finally to outright bitterness and despair.

Do not ask then, *"Are my grievances justified?"* Of course, they are, regarding the world and all the illusory cause-and-effect patterns that operate there. Your real question should be, *"Why am I continuing to invest this way?"* Because whenever you are holding grievances, you are professing the world is attacking me. So the ego thrives, and your belief in victimization strengthens. All your gripes and complaints and notions of injustice and persecution lead directly to acute mental toxicity, inner turmoil, firm dream identification and so much pandering after wasteful passions. They can lead to sickness, suicide, death and rebirth.

Let the no-mind state of Bodhicitta be your tranquil and relaxing sanctuary in the center of the storm of life. Strive to realize the mental quiescence that harbors no attachments. So will you be emancipated from the entire world of appearances! So will you find the quiet, serene eye in the hurricane of life! One that further potentiates and vitalizes you, with each passing hour! That restful influential center that produces no fluctuations of thought. One that will awaken you from all dreams and ferry you directly into Nirvanic Bliss.

As you relinquish all grievances and replace them with thoughts of gratitude and forgiveness, you uncover the light within. Forgiveness is the holy means to Salvation and the exact opposite of the ego's plan of holding grievances. Forgiveness reinstates you to your sacred powerhouse. It teaches, this dark cloud you perceive is unreal and cannot prevent you from reaching your inheritance. Once you begin to forgive vigilantly all sources of grievance, the dark cloud of gloom and doom atrophies in your mind. The ego starts becoming extinct. You comprehend this cloud is powerless to hold you back. It will remain forever insubstantial, for it is impotent to arrest even a feather's fall.

LINKING DIMENSIONAL EXPERIENCE TO OUR INWARD EVOLUTION

(Sharon) You said previously that dogs and other animals cannot experience a 3-D world because they cannot think in concepts. **How does our inner evolution affect our dimensional experience?**

(Jesus) There is an immediate and direct relationship between one's level of conscious evolution and the apparent dimensionality of one's world experience. Lower order organisms like bacteria, snails, and various forms of marine life, etc. which are only capable of sensory based experience get limited to a world, which has a very one-dimensional (1-D) quality to it. They experience their existence serially as if they are spending their whole lives moving along a line.

Whether the snail moves up a branch, or along the ground, the 2-D and 3-D realities that surround it, are very much invisible to it. This is because its degree of conscious experiencing has not evolved yet to include percepts and concepts. It can only experience these worlds as a series of changing stimuli. So, instead of saying snails, bacteria, microscopic cells etc. have a lower order consciousness, it is probably more accurate to say that once consciousness gets restricted to a limited range of sensation and vibration, this manifests into the life experiences of snails, bacteria, cells, sea polyps and other lower organisms.

The dog is higher up on the evolutionary chart since it can distinguish both sensations and percepts. A percept is just a group of different sensations lumped together as one whole. So even though oranges differ slightly in size, taste, color and smell, their underlying commonality overpowers their differences. This allows us to group them together under the banner of a single percept.

So the dog and higher lifeforms are forever scanning the larger field of their perception and breaking it up into individual percepts. Each such percept they react to and treat as wholes in themselves. For example, the percept of a bone may cause it to salivate, while that of a car may cause it to bark. So even though a bone and a car may be both hard objects and even share the same color, it views them as entirely different. Likewise, it knows man perceptually, but not conceptually. The dog, therefore, possesses a 2-D quality to its consciousness.

When it navigates through its 2-D world, it experiences various percepts as shrinking and growing. It cannot know their size is very often static and fixed, from the perspective of 3-D space. So a moving car, for example, can seem a very "alive" and threatening percept, in the dog's world. So even at those times, when it is resting comfortably on the grass, it will still run out and bark at a car. For the same reason too, it will often bark at its own reflection in the mirror.

Likewise, the out of sight is very much out of its mind. So the dog is very much living always in the NOW. It cannot conceive that there may be a gang riot going on in LA, while it is snoozing in its kennel. Its 2-D world experience flattens its picture. This means that it will never conceive of its body as actually extended in space. Its tail must often seem like one of the most alive and unpredictable novelties in its perceptual world. It perceives it as a foreign and invasive entity that is actively teasing it. That is why dogs sometimes run around erratically in circles seeking to bite at their own tails.

Because animals cannot think in terms of concepts, they will never accept an IOU in place of a tangible reality. No self-respecting monkey will snatch for the IOU instead of an actual banana. Nor will a dog accept an IOU for two bones tomorrow in place of a real one right now. Maybe we should do the same, so as not to suffer from mental breakdowns based on the future value of various derivative markets.

One could likewise argue that when consciousness gets restricted to a limited range of sensory and perceptive capabilities, this manifests as the 2-D life experiences of various animals. As long as one is incapable of thinking in concepts, one remains bound to a world that has a 2-D quality or lower. To understand this better, just take some picture or object in your room and carefully examine it. Now subtract all your conceptual understandings about it away. If you have done so correctly, you will realize, all that remains is a particular blend of texture and color and possibly a trace of some scent. In other words, what's left is a 2-D percept.

Without conceptual understanding, all becomes flattened because all its 3-D aspects are inferentially ascribed and arise from your conceptual thinking capability. Concepts are not intrinsic to the objects themselves. Conceptual understanding is like an overlay placed on our world that builds the 3-D quality into it.

CONCEPTS AND THE 3-D LANDSCAPE

(Sharon) So how did our conceptual thinking abilities arise?

(Jesus) The development of the conceptual thinking capability emerges with our capacity to see the underlying commonality between varying percepts. So even though, at a perceptual level, cars can seem very different in terms of color, shape, and size, we can still distinguish their underlying commonality. For instance, all cars possess an engine, four wheels, and an exhaust. Most feel cold, hard and metallic to the touch. Our concept of car lumps together all their common characteristics, rather than their divergent ones.

This ability to see the underlying commonalities provided us with a new edge. One that had the power to change the entire face of our existence. It afforded us with the capability to communicate through language and symbols. A single symbol or concept could be used to group together many incredibly diverse percepts. Symbolic thinking made mathematics and various phenomenal beliefs possible. For the first time, we began to conceive of ourselves as separate objects in our world. So our concept of an "**I**," as some separate self, arose. Soon we began to associate and bind various trains of thought to this "**I**." Since such thought-trains were extended through time, past and future became part of our experience. Only then did mental diseases began to proliferate as did a host of other typically human characteristics including ambition, greed, and wild notions of victimization.

Likewise, did the concepts of birth and death creep in for the first time, as did a new awareness of our identity. Our experience of existence was no longer held captive to the present moment and the field of our immediate perceptions. We were able to make conjectures into our future and also relive certain experiences from our past, at will. We could even bring our focus to dwell on various hypothetical worlds.

In contrast, dogs and other animals react to the field of their immediate perceptions, conditioned memories and conditioned patterns of response. Everything is happening now for the dog since it has no conception of a *before* and *after*. This safeguards it from becoming psychologically sick. The dog cannot temporally project since it has no concept of time. It cannot know, "*I am going to die.*" All it can feel is itself gradually weakening, losing appetite and zest for life on a moment-by-moment basis. Nor does it know it was born. Its predominate concern is gaining immediate gratification in the present.

If you point your fingers towards to the moon, the dog will never understand you. It cannot comprehend, that you are merely employing the fingers, to represent a reality beyond them. That is why the Buddha held up a flower and waved it about, in determining who was the most worthy disciple to pass on the Dharma line of transmission. With this single act, the Buddha was saying, "*I and this flower and everything in your field of perception has never been outside you. It is all just an imaginary landscape born from within.*"

Only Mahākāśyapa could understand this, and in that instant he became ecstatic. The peculiar, out of place motion of the flower, was a wordless communication directing him to go back within. He immediately apprehended that all was mind. That the flower and the Buddha were appearances of mind and never outside him. The essence of the Buddha was deathless and sharing this essence, so was he. Now he understood also that this realm of the transient, is illusory and has no Being. Real Being exists beyond all these illusions, including those of birth and death. Our immortal Self can never be compromised, in any way.

So, you must be beginning to grasp how your "*outer*" dimensional experience just reflects your degree of inner self-knowledge. At any given level of psychological evolution, you can perceive all the dimensions below your own cognitive levels, but not those above. An animal that suddenly learns to think in concepts will be enlightened out of the animal realm and experience a 3-D world. This launches it instantaneously, through an evolutionary shift forward, that can be considered a pivotal breakthrough in its consciousness. It will have migrated away from a reactive mode of consciousness that seeks immediate gratification to a more self-referential one can be far more calculating. For the first time, it will gladly accept IOUs and become a bean counter.

For humanity to experience higher dimensional existences, it must likewise transcend the limitation of concepts. It must begin to glimpse the underlying commonality and unity in all. Not only in that which it perceives but also in that which it conceives. So will each come to the silent tacit realization that the entire world of their perception and conception is in no way separate from themselves, their core beliefs and states of consciousness. Then it must dawn on us, that all these bodies that populate our world together with all their strange behaviors and needs are not so different after all. They are just variations on a common theme and composed of the same essential essence. All is Self! We must become potentiated to discern the underlying content of fear in a host of varying afflictions including depression, sickness, greed, attack, apathy, etc.

Likewise, we must come to know Love in all its many glorious faces. See it as the essential bedrock behind gratitude, inclusion, kindness, happiness, open-mindedness, etc. Doing so, our current experiences of time being serial in nature will fade, for we will have evolved to seeing its spatial character.

THE LIMITATIONS OF SYMBOLIC COMMUNICATION

(Sharon) How do our conceptual learning limitations affect the duration of our journey in Spacetime?

(Jesus) As you are aware by now, you have never been in spacetime, so your conceptual limitations can only hinder your capacity to grasp your true Identity. You are forever wasting time bartering in concepts and beliefs that can be constrictive, untrue or misleading. This unfortunate handicap can place you on the snail's path towards Truth because the limitations of symbolic and conceptual understanding can work as much against you, as for you.

You must quickly dispose of all that is pure rubbish and learn those precious criteria by which to assess the worthiness of a concept. For example, your concepts of separation and the body are invented lies; that your ego is invested in. All ideas that derive from such strange notions are therefore likewise untrue. This includes your concepts of bodily organs, metabolism, sickness, and death. The body is just a learning device, and it only appears because of your conditioned expectation and beliefs in separation.

Like all learning devices, it is neutral and incapable of learning. Just as a bicycle cannot learn to cycle by itself. So your mind must direct itself intelligently, to undo this illusion rather than strengthen it.

Symbolic thinking though infinite in its variety is yet very limited in its quality and scope. It permits only very infantile forms of communication. It is not an instantaneous and meaningful transmission because it depends on the serial arrangements of words. Words, in turn, can and will deceive because they are not the Truth. As I said in the Course, words are symbols of symbols and thus twice removed from truth. That is why you can download a hundred thousand of them at a shot for 99c on Amazon.

> **"Let us not forget, however, that words are but symbols of symbols. They are thus twice removed from reality."**
>
> [ACIM, MFT-21.1:9-10]

(Sharon) Yes, I can see just how empty and worthless words are simply by surfing through some social media sites like Facebook and Twitter. It seems everyone is a guru now and use words indiscriminately to spin a mesmerizing web of deception around themselves and others. Words are often used as a key defense against change or else to create the illusion that one is living their life. It is easy to talk about compassion and solidarity, but another thing entirely to implement it into action. Or to jabber about climbing Everest, as a deflection strategy from engaging the actual adventure. Many toss so many glowing and elevated words about but fail to exemplify them in their behaviors. When it comes to reviewing their own story, we find instead, a very stifling, contradictory and soul-crushing tale, elicited from a bifurcated tongue.

Many are false prophets who dare not swallow the poisonous concoctions they so freely disseminate. These, their disciples, graciously imbibe, as if it were, the ambrosia nectar of the gods. It is often those, who are most selfish, self-absorbed, psychotic and abusive who spout legions of empty euphonic sounding words promoting empathy, charity, and greater understanding. Yes, the psychic-vampires are everywhere draining our positive energy and lifeblood. So many, who just want to be spoon-fed their entire lives. In my mind's eye, I see them all there in their diapers, with a soother in their mouths contaminating the very air the rest of us need to breathe. They never take any effort to understand things for themselves and are contagiously heartless and unconscientious when it comes to the needs of others. None blazes their own path with an admirable fortitude. Instead, their whole approach is imitative and mimetic. They follow like deer in the footsteps of others.

Their bias and closed-mindedness enable so many foolish ideologies to flourish, and they are all suckers for media propaganda. Then the suckers fall prey to the self-victimized, so forming the toxic relationship of the sucker and the leach. The net effect is these pestilential and pathogenic psychodynamics expose us all to those collective consequences of paranoia, war, pandemics, etc. that follow from misinformation proliferation and destructive codependent relationships. As a result, genocides catch-on like the hula hoop, and there are always witch-hunts cratering out of the mob influence.

(Jesus) Yes, the only true messenger is one who has lived the message for himself. Only he deserves our ears and veneration. Otherwise, it can just be empty words sold by charlatans, frauds, and cheats. Unfortunately, the world has no ears, nose or eyes anymore — just a mouth that continuously flaps. That is why most will head directly into the path of a Tsunami, outfitted with their camera and i-

Phone, while the animals are leaving in droves. Man has lost all instinct, intuition, and smell and is sold fast on all that is superficial and meretricious.

Words have such appeal to him and so he keeps on yacking nonsensically with his motor lips as if it were going out of fashion. Even when his mouth shuts temporarily, his mind and thought keep chattering and gossiping within like a perpetual motion machine. His eyes are intractably sold on those tawdry attractions and desires of the world, and he stealthily avoids all to his distaste. He has become self-gouged by his impure motives and Machiavellian mind.

He does not fully cognize that mere words and symbols are powerless to reach certain higher realms. Symbolic thinking is often the crucial barrier that blinds. Nonetheless, such realms are of tremendous importance, as they portend vastly accelerated learning potential. Ultimate reality, remains beyond all our symbols and concepts. The consequence of this is that it also transcends all images and forms.

"As nothingness cannot be pictured, so there is no symbol for totality. Reality is ultimately known without a form, unpictured and unseen."

[ACIM, T-27.III.5:1-2]

All symbols and concepts establish boundaries on that which is Whole. That is why they are incapable of reaching to or containing truth directly. They can be envisioned as signposts or fingers that can point to the moon. However, just looking at a map, isn't going to take you to the destination. So you must be willing to change in order to arrive at Truth. Remember always that which is All, imposes no boundaries and therefore cannot be symbolized.

HUMANITY'S DECEPTION

(Sharon) Many would claim that our highly evolved capacity for using concepts and symbols was pivotal to our progressive development.

(Jesus) They were a stepping stone; that is all. Unfortunately, man, in his vanity and haughty contempt, mistakenly thinks now he is close to the peak of his evolution. He is merely at the summit of the Mons Venus. As he peers out at his world, he perceives all beings as below him on the evolutionary ladder. So he goes about with an unwarranted sense of superiority.

However, one must judge and evaluate a progressive evolution within by that which it produces without. So what is this picture that you see? Isn't one of great turmoil, greed, conflict, and fear! A world in which self-interest, callous disregard, and exclusion alone seem to rule! A world that is supremely unhappy and lost! What humanity does not recognize yet is that this cruel, and devastating image is its self-portrait. You may remember these words I spoke.

"The world is but a bridge; pass over it, but

build no houses on it."

[Famed inscription on the Buland Darwaza]

The same could be trumpeted about man. "*Man is but a bridge; Pass over him but build no houses upon him.*" Soon, he will need to either evolve or else he will regress back down into the slime. One thing is for sure; he cannot stay where he is, for much longer! If he does not heed the right evolutionary decisions, he will spiral rapidly downwards into lesser forms of creature-hood. There he could remain frozen for eons, as some Ötzi figurine, who is powerless to jumpstart himself.

(Sharon) Yes, it is now becoming increasingly self-evident that he is profoundly sick and empty. A blight on all creatures around him. He goes about raping, pillaging and poisoning all in his purlieu to build superficial toys to assuage his boredom. Even so, he will not even think of entering and mastering his inner domain of thought.

THE TREACHERY OF THE "I" CONCEPT

(Sharon) Can you explain how our I-concept develops and some of the problems that arise from it?

(Jesus) So much nonsense accumulates around this "I" concept during any given lifetime. It puts on such a dazzling show that we begin to believe these psychodramas are real and embody true living. Nonetheless, these charades represent nothing but a mind-generated fiction, and the "I" remains as a phantomlike presence; that seems hopelessly embedded in the machine of the world. An illusion, perpetuated out the ego's thought because the ego wholeheartedly believes it is separate.

The "I" resembles a snowball because it starts out as nothing but soon grows, as one pushes it uphill against the forces of spiritual gravity. It matures out of all our accumulated ignorance! Around this self-concept, we attach all our worldly ideas, fallacious beliefs, desires, merits and memories. With time it ripens into something every sophisticated, cultivated and vilely calculating. It fools all with its endless displays of culture, class and color.

Meanwhile, the ego being forever possessive and control-ling arbitrarily relegates this self to the partition of the body. It designates all that is behind this illusory boundary as the "**I**" and all that is outside, as the "**NOT-I**." It ignores the simple fact that the "**I**" is entirely dependent on the "**NOT-I**" both to know and sustain itself. Just think how ri-diculous the body would be, with no world of perception as its backdrop. It would be immersed in an ocean of noth-ingness, and one would have no worldly mirror, by which to improve on their understandings and values.

However, the ego is very bummed out by this state of af-fairs because the "**NOT-I**" is continuously disturbing its agenda and laying siege to its illusions of self-autonomy. It is perpetually entering the castle to wage war and aiming to destroy all those carefully crafted defenses; it has erect-ed, to protect itself. It is as if the "**NOT-I**" is staunchly de-claring, *"You cannot remain separate from your real Self for long, anymore than a bubble can remain apart from the ocean."* So it keeps on reminding the ego that its "**I**" cannot stand up to the laws of truth indefinitely because the "**I**" and the "**NOT-I**" are really one.

The ego's game-plan is to distract your attention from this raw understanding. So it hides and schemes and sneers behind its wall of flesh where everything festers and rots and nothing ever grows. It has you sign on the dotted line, a manifesto of loyalty, which then waives all your rights and privileges. Then it coerces you into accepting its terrifying picture as your reality. Nevertheless, the terms of its agreement can change on a moment-to-moment basis as demanded by the ceaseless flux of its own capricious desires, torments, and anxieties. Over time, due to the mass hypnotizing power of conditioning you begin to believe in the ego's lies. You begin to differentiate yourself from all those around you and to judge harshly, all that remain outside the fence of your body. Thus you guarantee this wicked landscape of separation will endure.

So what can you do now, but tramp aimlessly about, impregnated with a deep discomfort and uncertainty in your being; feeling ravished in your heart and swamped by a torrent of icy emotions. Disconnected and isolated, you know something is amiss but for the life of you, you cannot figure it out. Having lost access to the Holy Vision which alone can set you free, you bend so easily to all the ego's evil games.

THE DISTORTIONARY POWER OF THE CONCEPTUAL

(Sharon) Is conceptual understanding useful or an impediment?

(Jesus) Concepts are mind-made phantoms we arbitrarily superimpose over the plenum of the void. They are utilized, to extract some form of meaning from our perceptions and to identify causal connections in our spatiotemporal existence. Unfortunately, they operate by breaking the whole into parts, and each concept introduces its own distortions. They are like the cookie-cutters of the mental realm because they establish artificial boundaries, where none are to be found. These particular cookie-cutters, however, are shaped by all our beliefs and mental incapacities. They can be mobilized as useful learning aids or else to cripple all progress. Mistaken conceptual understandings can easily beach us indefinitely on the shores of unreality.

Nevertheless, they can become so generalized, clear and potent as to point almost directly to the transcendent Realm. By properly culturing and grooming our minds they place us in a perfect readiness state for Truth. Their ultimate end purpose is to help us evolve beyond any need for them.

(Sharon) It is not clear to me how concepts create boundaries and distort. Can you provide some examples?

(Jesus) Our minds are flooded with literally millions of concepts, on a daily basis. We have concepts of our identities, purpose and even of for the underlying meaning of our past experiences. We hold concepts of the divine and also of the Anti-Christ. Concepts, for what we consider loving and good, as well as for that we regard as fearful and evil. We have exploitive concepts aimed at destroying the world we appear to live in — the type of concepts that lead to nuclear bombs. We are attracted to those who fit with our concepts of beauty, virtue, and intelligence. Our idea of beauty can be very limiting. It most typically emerges from the possession of certain attributes, such as having blond hair, blue eyes, and a wholesome body. Anyone who does not rigorously meet these standards is placed outside the boundary and considered as either plain or outright ugly. But in truth, beauty exists on a spectrum and what is one man's prize may be another man's poison.

Similarly, our concept of intelligence is often rooted in the inheritance of certain competencies such as creativity, ingenuity, wizardry, or powers of abstraction. We fail to see that intelligence exists along a spectrum and is very multidimensional in nature. Another may base their concept of intelligence on adaptability, memory capacity, sports talent or communicative power. For example, many consider some of our politicians to be intelligent because of their abilities to rapidly flip and adapt while communicating nonsense and lies so artfully, through unblinking eyes. The startling fact that such politicians are often glaringly deficient or completely barren in the powers of reason, creativity, ingenuity, and abstraction seems to make not, a whit of difference.

Nevertheless, we roam about our world attaching all sorts of invisible labels to all we see. Labels built-up from the nebulous haze of all our conceptual ideations. Very quickly the greater mass of humanity becomes divided into millions of separate entities whose degree of isolation is motivated by how they fit in with all our conceptual filters. The concepts we hold do not exist in a vacuum. They are very active in both fashioning and interpreting all that we see. It is like they superimpose an invisible mesh or graticule on the world of our perceptions. One that then sorts, divides and classifies into discrete entities, that which is in fact, a single continuum. What we do not realize is this mesh is highly distortionary and a wholly unnecessary encumbrance.

Consequently, someone who does not have one of our desired attributes for intelligence may suddenly find themselves boxed in on the wrong side of this mesh, where they are now categorized as worthless or even repulsive. This mesh is applied to everything and includes people, animals, hobbies, careers, food, investments and so on. Likewise, we apply it to all that we find addictive and worth pursuing or avoid like the plague. In fact, anything we can see or even conceive will be quantized by this mesh. It very much forges and shapes the world into its likeness. It is only when we dismantle it, that we can come into contact with the undifferentiated potency and wisdom of the Void and realize the world of true perception.

Concepts are not born in the Void. They are driven from within ourselves. They are mental images that carry and embed all our beliefs, prejudices, judgments, and limitations. Inner mental images that are then projected outward to cut our world into pieces. We will experience a dark, hostile circumvented world whenever our concepts are not in alignment with Truth. Light enters our perceptions to the extent that all our partially veracious concepts are remolded into harmony with Truth and all our ego based concepts are driven out.

Concepts present us with distorted slices and fragmentations of what is Whole, but these slices are somewhat useless on their own. Eventually, we need to glimpse that meaningful transcendent picture which connects all the dots. For example, one can be shown pictures of a complex design from many different angles and still never mentally induct or visualize the unified design. One must grasp first, how the individual elements come together and how they are meaningfully related. So it is with concepts. Each shares meaningful connections with numerous others that may seem so very different. When you have seen the complete design, you will no longer need to bother with concepts. For who persists in looking at the fingers once they have finally beheld the majesty of the moon?

It is a grave mistake to consider any concept as complete in itself. Rather look at the common elements shared between them and use this to either expand or transcend them. Capture or intuit their underlying message and see how this same content is reflected in other concepts as well. Only then will you move upwards in the elevator of mind and experience a world of an entirely different dimension and quality.

Then the projected universe explodes with something entirely new and fresh and permeated with meaning. This meaning was forever latent and only awaiting a subtle but immense improvement in your psychic-evolutionary capabilities, to be exposed. Now the dreamer pictures through vision a world, far more attuned to truth. He no longer needs even the concept of the body, by which to learn.

"The time will come when you will not return in the same form in which you now appear, for you will have no need of it. Yet now it has a purpose, and will serve It well."

[ACIM, WB.157.7:3-4]

THE POWER OF THINKING SMARTLY

(Sharon) How can we best plan for Success?

(Jesus) It has been asserted, that the person of genius is most active and potent exactly at that moment when he seems to be doing absolutely nothing. **Learn from this!** Just a few flashes of intelligent thought and reflection, and unbiased reason can save lifetimes of mistakes and futile wandering. This is the real thinking smartly. As I said before:-

> **"Meaningful seeking is consciously undertaken, consciously organized and consciously directed. The goal must be formulated clearly and kept in mind."**
>
> [ACIM, T-4.V.6:3-4]

One with a prodigious and untainted capacity for inductive reasoning can easily elicit into view, that which with the body's eyes can never behold. Such a short investment, of your time, can place you in a mental readiness state to experience worlds of a much higher dimension. In contrast, your actions can often feel very agonizing, hopeless and unnecessary when you are operating in a lower dimensional context. Your feelings of frustration and anxiety can escalate in such a fragmented landscape because you do not really know what you are doing.

Likewise, you are blind to the vast cascade of effects streamlining from your every thought, decision and action. Nor know the wisest and quickest path that serves your best interests.

Hence, like the pupa of a butterfly you painfully crawl about, taking forever to get the tiniest distance. Unless you go through an inner metamorphosis, you will never fly with the grace and ease that your divinity entrusts to you. Increased apathy and joylessness, can be the first signs that you are finally ready to advance. For you have seen through all idols and fantasies, cherished in your past. Seen how tarnished and lackluster they are and so possessed of an underlying emptiness. Once you recognize the infinite paths to failure and despair, they set you on; you will gladly trade-in all your masks of specialness and deception to launch in an entirely new direction.

ADVENTURING INTO THE SUPRA-CONCEPTUAL

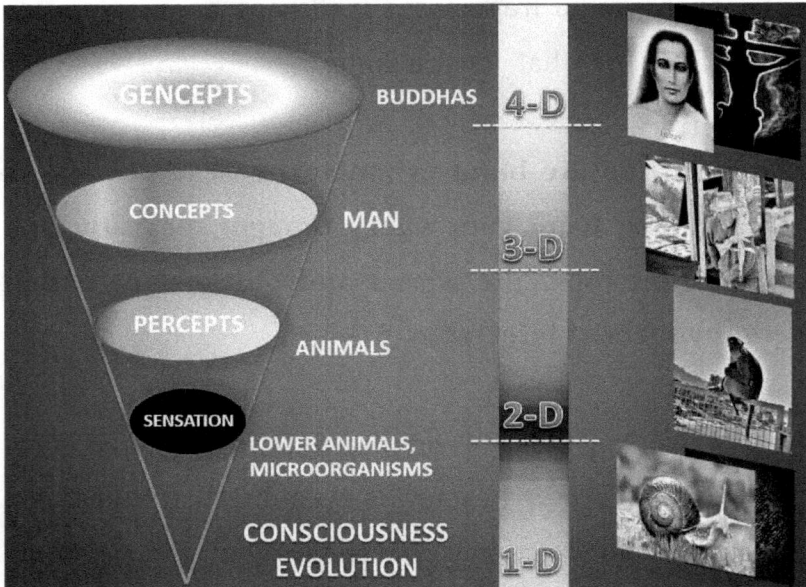

THE CRITICAL PHASES IN THE EVOLUTION OF CONSCIOUSNESS

(Sharon) What are some of the fundamental changes needed?

(Jesus) Just as the next psychic-evolutionary step for the dog is to move from percepts to concepts. **The next evolutionary step for man is deciphering the realm of the supra-conceptual. This radical leap will take him into unknown and unchartered territories.** Nonetheless, he will be presented with a world that remains backward compatible with all that he has formerly known. It can be considered an organic superset of what went before. One in which he enters an entirely higher modality of experiencing his true being.

For example, a butterfly does not lose, what it knew as a larva or pupa when it undergoes its glorious metamorphosis. However, once it evolves into a butterfly, it can easily travel vast distances with beauty, grace, and elegance. For it has gained the majestic wings by which to gambol effortlessly about. What demanded enormous expenditures of energy and effort before, is now experienced so painlessly. The butterfly has simply gained the higher perspective. All the same, when we look closely, we see it is traveling in the exact same space that it did before, as a pupa. It is now just doing it with such exquisite beauty.

Likewise, the higher reality for man will still be inclusive of concepts, percepts, and sensations. However, his mind will have transcended, these very limited representations of reality and be potentiated with immeasurably new powers. For who bothers with an abacus once he has learned algebra and calculus? Once we experience the leap into the supra-conceptual, we will no longer be held ransom and restricted to very crippling modes of experiencing our existence. We will know the entire symbiotic relationship that exists between our mind and its many reflections in the mirror of the world. Our Divine Identity will become revealed from this higher vantage point, and all superior relationships known.

We will instantaneously capture the full monumental effects and recursive regressions streaming from our mildest and innocuous decisions. Objects, functions and phenomena will be displaced like the abacus of old. We will no longer limit our communication through them, as we now do. Objects will be overtly known as illusory apparitions arising from a set of interdependent relationships. All classical theories of separation and objective existence will be seen as the immature thoughts of a puerile mind.

The classical-orientated mind-frame functioned by assigning very specific cause-and-effect relationships to all aspects of its world. It often habitually confused the two and inverted true relationships. For example, it taught that objects give rise to phenomena, but it is more accurate to say that phenomenal interactions produce the notion of an object. An even higher understanding comprehends that mind alone gives rise to all appearances. This higher evolution is concurrent with a migration away from the tedious land of specifics to engage a breathtaking open-ended world of abstracts. The holy pinnacle from which we become transported into the presence of Truth.

THE RETURN OF THE ANCIENT ONE

(Sharon) What will this Higher Realm be Like?

(Jesus) The new world that awaits is yet an ancient one. It has always been here but requires an evolution of mind to be revealed. As man ascends, he will uncover his original essence. He will be shuttling at greatly accelerated speeds to the beginning of time. As I have said before:-

"Truly, truly, I say to you, before Abraham was born, I am."

[John 8:58]

That is because I stand at the very entrance point to Truth and at that portal where the illusion of time begins. Abraham, on the other hand, still had some lessons to fine-tune and resolve before he could return to the beginning. Here, at last, is the holy place where all illusions come to an end. That is why I declared *"I am the Alpha and the Omega, the first and the last, the beginning and the end. Blessed are those who wash their robes, so that they may have the right*

to the tree of life, and may enter by the gates into the city...."
[Revelations 22:13-14]

Where is the beginning and end of time, except at the Eternal Now! One is the *Alpha and the Omega* only when they have come full circle, and their knowledge is complete. Then they are restored to a state of mental purity that sits undefiled because they have washed their robes of all erroneous thought and mistaken beliefs. They, therefore, are aware of their original purity and innocence, and this bestows on them the right to enter the City of Eternity. This, they then enter by the gate of the **Eternal Now**. Along the way, all that was illusory and deceptive will be falling away. Even memories will be reorganized and flushed of all that represented mere ego hallucinations.

Man has swum far too long, on the surface of the mind while avoiding the mysteries of the deep. To reach again, the ancient and the timeless, his understandings needs to be forged back into alignment with formless knowledge. The ice of his conditionings and the restrictions imposed by his very specific thought processes need to be blown out and melted. In this holy firmament, he must become the blacksmith on himself. Only so, can all false time-based beliefs, be expunged from the mind, so that the transcendent reality may emerge, once more, from the mists. His way becomes easy and clear, as he removes all ego obstructions. The Ancient Home he is searching form existed prior to concepts, percepts, and sensations. These are just worldly overlays that distort it. To enter the gates, he must step away from these very limited modes of functioning. He must no longer be fooled by that bleak picture which his senses portray to him because this sensory world can only ever image his beliefs. He must fully recognize that what appears different can yet be the same, just as what appears the same, can yet be different.

All apparent differences are just many different faces on a single higher order essence. To know, this requires a Titanic development in his current psychic functioning. An evolutionary shift in his consciousness so that the common content and life-force behind all form can be revealed. Once he trains himself to think differently, he will perceive differently. Because, in the final analysis, all his perceptions crystallize out of his beliefs.

GENCEPTS

(Sharon) You have emphasized that the next evolutionary step in man's consciousness is the progression to the supra-conceptual. Can you provide more insight on this?

(Jesus) Percepts and concepts are those developmental capabilities that made the 2-D, and 3-D world experiences possible. Gencepts are that latent developmental capability, which will reveal the 4-D world to him. These represent a fundamental shift to a higher mode of his psychic-functioning.

(Sharon) Sorry, but I have never heard the term gencept before!

(Jesus) Yes, I have had to invent the term because your worldview is not sufficiently advanced, as to be aware of them. You cannot fathom their presence, anymore than a parasitic fish knows that is living its entire life on the back of a whale. Gencepts represent very broad and generalized understandings that are deeply threaded to reality. They represent our supra-conceptual thinking capabilities. You cannot picture them because they are witnessed only by a mind that is capable of attaining to far higher levels of abstraction. Once you can comprehend and recognize their presence, your learning progress will accelerate immeasurably.

GENCEPTS REPRESENT INFINITE FIELDS OF POTENTIALITY

One can think of gencepts as representing an array of conceptual understandings or an entire field of potentialities, all at once. Gencepts embody all such potentialities within themselves, just as a polygon embodies all multi-sided figures. As you know, a polygon is far more abstract than any of its specific implementations. It is therefore of a higher potency since it simultaneously contains and yet transcends all its manifestations.

Likewise, gencepts are immanent and transcendent to the world you now perceive. They represent a higher integration category that rises far above all concepts, percepts, and sensations; you are currently aware of. You can think of any individual world perception or experience, as just one face of a gencept. The gencept, however, like the mythical Hydra has many heads. Two entirely different concepts or ideas can share a single gencept. In fact, a single gencept can connect the dots between tens of thousands of concepts, all at once.

It can quickly reveal what very distinct concepts, taken alone and in isolation, are powerless to portray. It can highlight instantaneously all the dependencies and commonalities existing between very divergent concepts or ideas. One can think of them as tracing and imaging the deeper relationship interconnecting very diverse conceptual ideas, into a single view.

GENCEPTS AND ASSOCIATIVE VIEWING

(Sharon) I still cannot quite grasp them!

(Jesus) That is because your entire world experience is based on serialized, rather than associative viewing. In consequence, your life experiences, unfold to you slowly, one 3-D view at a time. So your learning is fundamentally linear in nature. The full storyline is unnecessarily prolonged. You have to wait until the end of your life movie to find out what happens. Often, by that time, you can no longer clearly remember the frames that went before. Time erodes the clarity causing you to lose sight of the tighter interactions and meaning. Nor can you see the full long term impact your decisions have on the lives of others. This is one of the principal reasons most are so indecisive and riddled with anxiety. Those wise enough, recognize that they do not know what the hell they are doing.

Associative viewing, in contrast, is far more powerful. It would be like taking all the frames from a movie and instantly displaying them on an array of screens simultaneously. But doing so in a manner that emphasizes all their interconnections and critical content correlations. So you would be empowered to take in the full movie instantaneously and grasp its underlying meaning and storyline. Thus, you preemptively avoid any time-wastage spent watching it. Associative viewing in not limited like serialized information transfer is. You can just as easily see all the frames for tens of thousands of movies and immediately extract the common themes and ideas that underlie or umbrella them all. So quickly capturing the entire field of outcomes that will eventuate from following certain ideas and decisions.

The associative power of a gencept goes even deeper. You are not limited just to images but can also associatively represent all sensory information. In fact, all potentialities emerging from a single idea can be associatively exhibited contemporaneously. For example, take the basic concept of a book. To you, a book is just a book! It is a rather flat representation in words of a storyline you may not even be remotely interested in. You often detest having to wade through so many words, just to get to the interesting and useful bits. Maybe it will just end up boring you to death. How many months or years of your life have you already lost this way?

The gencept, in stark contrast, will reveal all its information and core content, in an instant. So you will know all key ideas, concepts, nuances, emotional entanglements and mental and spiritual shifts of the key protagonists in the book upfront. But the scope goes far greater. You will also see all possibilities that will ever emerge for books. Everything from the printing press to modern e-readers, audio and video books to interactive books based on virtual reality technologies. You will be presented with books that can stimulate all your senses and be interactively lived through in highly immersive VR universes.

Imagine a book on cooking that enables you to smell, see and taste the final dish, in advance of cooking it. You will be very grateful to have been saved from making poor culinary decisions and wasting your hard-earned greenbacks purchasing the necessary ingredients. Nevertheless, this small example is just a minor rendering of this gencept's power. Another important qualitative dimension to gencepts is that they can function superlatively as the ultimate catalysts for driving innovation. Once you become trained to unearth them, you will have the intuitive eye for discerning linkages between diverse concepts that are not always self-evident on the surface.

For example, imagine if you were simply introduced to the concept of radio transmission, a century ago, and were then instantly shown all technologies that will ever emerge from this one idea or concept. You would be speechless because you would be immediately flooded with images of satellites, rockets, cable boxes, drones, i-phones, GPS base stations, transponders, cloud servers, gaming technologies, advances in medical imaging, cybernetics, robotics, monitoring devices, etc. You would have insight into what stocks to invest in and would no longer bother taking shorthand dictation notes for your boss.

(Sharon) These visualizations are interesting and somewhat compelling, but I still can't conceive of a gencept. They seem so elusive and intangible. Maybe you are just inventing a new term to represent something that does not exist.

(Jesus) Of course, you cannot conceive of a gencept, because they are not concepts, they are gencepts. They transcend concepts and even conceiving itself. You can only genceive gencepts. Think of this way; a dog cannot conceive of a car. It can only perceive a car. Failing to see the underlying commonality between cars, it perceives each one as totally unique. Therefore it cannot intuitively grasp what the concept of a car could possibly be referring to. For it, to conceive of a car, a whole new mode of experiencing is demanded of it. One in which it has a momentous epiphany and identifies the common threads in what appears as different.

(Sharon) But how can a host of divergent concepts be connected by a single gencept? The thread still seems invisible to me!

(Jesus) Take your capacity for sensation, as an example. You currently experience the sensations of touch, taste, smell, sound, shape, etc. as completely independent and separate realities. You see no connection between the number "5" and the color green or between the sound of E-flat from the color blue. But that is not the case for those with synesthesia. Different sensations come to them as inseparable and as one. They often will automatically associate different colors with certain numbers, letters, and words or associates particular tastes to various shapes, etc.

Some synesthetes have perfect five sense synesthesia and thus link all five sensations of shape, smell, sound, touch or taste in everything they experience. So a triangle, might, for example, be experienced as yellow, smell and taste like mango, sound like D-flat and feel very sharp and tingly to the touch. Thus, as you can well imagine, they often possess eidetic memories. Their world experience is very different from yours. What you experience, as completely different and separate, they experienced as highly merged and unified. All modes of their sensation are hopelessly and inextricably tangled as one.

GENCEPTS AND CROSS-POLLINATION

(Sharon) How can I identify the deeper common threads in concepts, so as to apprehend their parent gencept?

(Jesus) You have to look higher and deeper and extricate their common purpose. For example, you consider books and holographic imaging as completely different and independent concepts. It doesn't immediately register with you, that they are both forms of visual communication. This is just one of their common features. Grasping this, you start to discern the presence of an underlying gencept. One whose power transcends either of these forms of communication taken individually.

Thus, were you to create a book and image its words and fundamental ideas as holographic images, it would be much simpler to read and understand. You would be able to portray its dominant threads and essential content far more lucidly and effectively! You could empower it also with new features such as interactive storylines that facilitate the assimilation of its principal ideas and motifs.

You could cross-pollinate this approach to other domains as well. Alternatively, you could shape these themes through different filters, more suited to the reader's predilections and interests. For example, a book on Christianity might have its dominant ideas represented into holographic images that relate it to similar concepts in Zen, Taoism, Buddhism, Sufism, Zoroastrianism, Vedanta, Mohammedanism or whatever takes your fancy. You could also live out the key experiences of a book through the eyes of each of its dominant characters. Word imprints on a page often fail miserably to capture the very heightened emotion, stress or criticality of the decision making involved. Words depend on tedious and lengthy portraitures given by the Author. So one is always just projecting the emotional experience of the lead characters through one's imagination and powers of extrapolation.

Remember this is just an initial baby step. We have only summarily reviewed a single common thread running through two different concepts. As you extend this approach through numerous concepts and across multiple shared domains, the potency of the gencept is seen to grow exponentially. You will begin to see how the core content in one concept easily cross-associates and interacts with many other concepts.

Individual concepts in comparison will now seem so narrow-banded, flat and bounded when seen in isolation. You will begin to glimpse why you always failed to capture the bigger picture. Being zealously overly-focused on individual concepts was like trying to navigate your way in the world using Hansel and Gretel's breadcrumbs.

Let's take another example. This time, we are going to distill and extract all your associations to **Peace**. Peace, for instance, is a formless concept and yet a concept all the same. However, is it evident to you that the concept **"Peace**," is not the reality of **Peace**? Many are sold by their very superficial ideations on this concept. They believe they are experts, even though they may never have experienced the tiniest measure of true Peace. Like most, that are quickly bought and sold by the ego's cheap allurements and so often mistake the map for the real adventure. Now go meditate for five minutes and then relate all associations to peace, you have discovered.

5-Mins later

(Sharon) At first, I began to associate peace with a state of deep rest. But then, as I meditated a little longer, I began to associate it also with laziness, inactivity, and sleep. Soon more negative associations crept in such as apathy, callous indifference, sluggishness as well as impotence, stupidity, and ineptness. Then shortly after this, even more, ideas flooded in. I felt it was like being in a blissful state of ignorance, and thoughtlessness. Imbued with the tamasic temperament of deep inertia and withdrawal from the world.

(Jesus) You have not meditated very well. Only your first association to peace was accurate because peace does indeed induce deep rest. However, all your other associations are infiltrated, tainted and thoroughly suffused by all your worldly knowledge about peace. They bear no real connections to its underlying reality. Peace has nothing in common with being in a state of ignorance, thoughtlessness, inertia or withdrawal. These are ego articulations about it. In fact, the true connections are almost the exact opposite of those you have spoken.

In contrast, peace has everything in common with boundless energy, wakefulness, creativity, potency, flawless action, and extreme intelligence. It is an active power that infuses one with tremendous vitality, perfect understanding, and a restful state of mindfulness. When one is truly in an unassailable state of peace, they can feel, their authentic being as an uncontainable field of quiet energy which cannot be disturbed. You encounter no obstructions but merge seamlessly with all. Yes, genuine peace is a very positive and active endowment and one that can only bless. This tiny depiction of Peace is what illuminated yogis have always been hinting at when they describe the bliss of being in a pure Sattvic temperament.

Unconditional Peace is also your natural state. However, this natural state can only be unveiled by being sincerely honest and truthful in what you really know and engaging the world with an open impartial mind. This necessitates dropping all your futile defenses and protections and communicating sincerely instead with all those around you. Peace cannot be reached by hibernating away and separating yourself from existence or by avoiding all risks. Nor can it be achieved by cherishing unrealistic dreams or seeking to exploit others. Ask yourself, "*Do I come to forgive or to condemn? To help or to hinder? To join or self–protect? To demand or to bless?*" and this will quickly reveal to you, why your state of mind is the way it is.

Now you fathom the crucial abstraction that unconditional peace does not emerge in a vacuum. It flowers from being thoroughly centered, even when bombarded by a maelstrom of insanities, personal demands, and frenzied calls for help. Madness and distraction provide the essential backdrop in which it can mature.

The reality of peace shares a deep connection with many other concepts, ideas, and creative life-forces. But we have lost the ability to discern these hidden connections and the underlying genceptual reality that is latent to them all. They became masked by our obsessive and exclusive focus on the world of specifics. For example, suppose you are out wandering alone in some hot, dusty and arid desert some-where in Utah, Colorado or New Mexico and stumble on some interesting and novel bone fragments. You may not ever recognize such bone fragments as the fossilized re-mains of some great dinosaur from the Triassic period. This is because the dinosaur's imprint is spread so vastly on the ground beneath your feet.

So often it is, that when we are in the presence of some-thing immense, powerful and world shattering, we cannot recognize it. Because what has become deeply embedded and yet so widespread, we often fail to discern and appre-hend. We have become blind to that which is omnipresent and intrinsic to every aspect of our perception.

THE TWO FUNDAMENTAL GENCEPTS

(Sharon) How many gencepts are there?

(Jesus) The designation of gencept can be applied to any group of tightly interconnected concepts that all share the same underlying content. For example, the ego, error and the dissociative condition known as split-mind all arise and go together. Fundamentally they are just different faces of a single gencept. Likewise, the body, the spacetime belief, and the grievance-laden mindstate are all intimately interdependent and therefore share the same parent gencept. When the mind reaches a superior level of abstraction, it recognizes the true nature of Reality. Then it also cognizes that there are just two fundamental gencepts.

1. **The Gencept of Truth**

2. **The Gencept of Error**

The Gencept of Truth

This gencept encompasses Wholeness, Timelessness, Creation, Love, Bliss, Peace, Reality, etc. All that is constant, radiant, self-perpetuating and changeless in the endless sea of change. The underlying essence of this gencept is Love and Totality because its power remains unopposed, its scope limitless and there is nothing real apart from it.

The Gencept of Error

This gencept has no power and can survive only in a world of illusion. Its underlying essence is that of nothingness. It embodies all that is transient and encompasses all mental miscreations born out of our ignorance, impurity, and distortionary beliefs. It strengthens whenever we lend our faith to the unreal and artificial. The gencept of error the parent gencept that gave birth to the ego, the spacetime artifice and all worlds of separation and form. As you invest conscious energy in it, you become unhappy, fearful and sick. You become displaced from your real Identity and start to believe in your own mind-generated hallucinations.

Feeling hopelessly immersed in a world of bodies you start to believe in the power of judgment, condemnation, and attack to get what you want. It is only natural, in this severely sickened and delusional mindstate that you will use every means possible to survive. Feeling apart and thoroughly victimized by the world you begin projecting crazy notions of guilt and sin to all around you. Thus identifying yourself as a prisoner of the world of form, you progress to begging your way through life, and no longer recognize the power of your thought. So you cave readily to so many addictions and psychological pleasures, and worldly idols that would never have tempted you before.

This gencept derives entirely out of wrong beliefs and first arose when you entertained the original error of the TMI. All the same, you can use the power of your free will to relinquish this gencept entirely from your mind. You just need to see how all its inherent aspects support one another and then renounce your support.

(Sharon) Thanks for the bigger picture. **Where does consciousness come into play in all this?**

(Jesus) Consciousness can be seen as somewhere in the middle. In fact, before we entertained the Gencept of Error at the time of the fall, we were not conscious at all. We knew only of the Gencept of Truth and were in direct contact with the Absolute. Operating seamlessly out of the

Knowledge of Whole-Mind, we were Creative and unimpeded by illusions. Consciousness, like the Relative Existence, is a mirage that arose from entertaining error. Consciousness is within what the Relative Existence is without. Both are fundamentally impure modes of experiencing your existence. Nevertheless, they can serve as a useful platform for your return to Knowledge. This can be accomplished by expunging error and its effects from your conscious belief. So does the world of form disappear and consciousness is returned to Whole-Mind.

(Sharon) How can we ever be Creative, if we are not Consciously Aware?

(Jesus) You still carry a very ego notion of awareness. The severely dissociated type. That of a sullied and defiled awareness, which only knows itself through all it has judged against and seen as separate. Pure awareness only exists at the level of Being. It arises from a state of immaculate knowing and of not feeling severed or disunited from any aspect of existence. Instead, one feels blissfully infused into all aspect of Creation in an altogether immersive orgasmic experience. Here there is no notion of any boundary, anywhere, or ever.

THE HOLISTIC NATURE OF GENCEPTS

(Jesus) Each aspect of a gencept contains the essence of the whole. So all ideas and concepts in a gencept chain are interrelated and share the same content. Every conceptual face or potentiality can be envisioned as just presenting a different window on the whole.

(Sharon) How can each aspect contain the Whole?

(Jesus) Gencepts have a lot in common with infinite number theory, because it is not a matter of degree, quantity and size but of purity, flexibility and power. In the Relative World the concept *Might makes Right* seems to carry tremendous meaning, However in Eternity, *Right makes Might* is seen to be the true order of things. For example, in infinite number theory, the part can be made into the whole by a minor operation such as multiplication or division. So the infinite set of even natural numbers 0,2,4,6,8,10, . . . can easily become the infinite set of natural numbers 0,1,2,3,4,5, . . . Simply by dividing each member of the former by 2. So it also with gencepts, you cannot separate the part from the whole, because they are one.

As a result, if you entrust your full faith to any concept or idea, that is part of a gencept, it will soon take you to the whole. Then all associated concepts and ideas will emerge from the woodwork because the same invisible thread links them all. It is just like an underground organization, in which finding one leak is sufficient to expose all members.

For example, if you have complete mental conviction in the reality of sin, it will be impossible not to believe in guilt also. The beliefs in sin and guilt flourish or die together like a band of blood brothers. Cherishing sin you will be automatically attracted to judgment, condemnation, and attack because these serve to keep all sins "alive and well," and beyond all question or doubt. So your mind works overtime discerning more evidence of sin, everywhere in your perception. This cements your landscape of separation securely into place. Meanwhile, feeling isolated and untrusting of everyone, it is not long before the world of fear emerges and becomes very real to you. You may not be consciously aware of how your entire world arises from your firm conviction to one belief or one idea, but it does!

Likewise, if you dislodge your faith in any aspect of this gencept, you can easily uproot it all. For example, if you no

longer extend your faith to sin, the foundation of guilt soon
loses its strongest and most loyal support. Seeing no one as
sinful, your senseless justifications for continued judgment, condemnation, and attack, now seem totally out of
place. As all boundaries between yourself and "others" dissolve, fear vaporizes as do all fear-based defenses. The
world of separation, serving no purpose likewise melts
away. The ego only seems to exist, to the extent that you
believe in the gencept of error. It will continue to do so
while you retain belief in any of its aspects.

Lending your faith instead to the gencept of Truth, you find
yourself traveling towards the Kingdom. As spiritual vision
becomes restored, your entire world experience changes
for the better. You feel yourself onboard a luxury cruise
liner that is journeying towards the boundless ocean of
Knowledge. Your ego scheduler and all its distractions having been tossed away, you simply relax and enjoy. Your increased experience of timelessness makes you more light-
hearted and carefree. Miracles become more profuse, in
your daily life and an aura of genuine happiness, calm and
joyous expectancy surround you. All because you decided
against that junkyard barge that was heading into the frozen Bering Straits towards those ego icebergs of ignorance,
objectivism, and form.

The purpose of spacetime, consciousness, and all learning devices is to facilitate your withdrawal from all beliefs encompassed by the gencept of error. The Atonement has the express mission of having you retain only those understandings, which are consistent with the gencept of Truth. When your faith to the gencept of Truth has gained your complete mental conviction, then your faith is needed no more. For then the relative existence will have completely disappeared.

DARKNESS AND THE GENCEPT OF ERROR

(Sharon) Why is there is much darkness and confusion and how do we release more light into our perceptions?

(Jesus) This false world of appearances is the direct result of man's self-induced slavery to the gencept of error. So he is seen frantically pacing about reacting to unstable perceptions, as programmed from the template of his erroneous beliefs. He remains unfulfilled only because of all those untruths; he has accepted.

Each perceptual frame he witnesses is a distortion of the real. They still contain aspects and shreds of what is whole, but his errors make him blind to their underlying wholeness. Thought purification is therefore needed to purge all their distortionary elements. Man's spacetime experiences can be interpreted as nothing more than a series of existential vignettes carved from a higher order reality. The many uncertain shadows he perceives, only arise from his lost access to the inner light. Unfortunately, he makes these unstable and fleeting appearances into his guides for decision and action. No wonder he cannot easily fathom what is in his best interests! Meanwhile, his ego has placed so many cruel sentinels at the gates to his unconscious that prevent him from gaining access to its wisdom.

To bring forth his true perceptions, once more, he must learn those criteria by which to clearly differentiate the entirely valuable and worthy from the worthless. Thus he will amplify only the real while divesting all else. When complete, he will have the vision of the perfect timeless unity that is everpresent. In the Course, I provided the principles for distinguishing the real from the worthless in Workbook Lesson 133 *"I will not value what is valueless."* Follow these then to help you make the correct evaluations.

(Sharon) Can you provide an example of applying these criteria?

(Jesus) All dreamers are attracted and distracted by the never-ending flood of tantalizing images appearing on the screen of the void. They see each such appearance as independent of their states of consciousness.

Man sees motion as a real property, instead of an emergent one arising from embracing incorrect views. So he does not grasp that all spacetime experiencing and form is a product of his distortions. He runs into the same fundamental issues again when trying to uncover the gencept of Truth. He tries futilely to connect the dots, in all that is illusory and ephemeral and aims to evaluate its worthiness through the murky haze of his mind. As I said in the Course, one should not search for the real in what is transient, because Truth being changeless obviates the world of time. There has never been any *"Where"* for anything to happen in, nor any *"Time,"* in which it could happen. Eternity remains Always, as do You! Only a mind sunk deep in ignorance, experiences change while one relinquished of it, experiences only the changelessness of Nirvana.

Look to all that is transient and which serves no useful purpose to diagnose the unreal. Sickness, suffering, loss and death serve no purpose, so they cannot be real. The body perpetually changes, so it is likewise an apparition of mind. The purpose of sin, guilt, judgment and attack is separation. So such practices and endorsements are thinly veiled ego attempts to prove the illusory is reality. This, of course, is impossible! So waste no more time there.

Applying this rationale and decimating thinking approach rigorously to all values and beliefs, you currently esteem, transports you in the right direction. So do you recognize, the dualism implicit in consciousness arises from your complicity to error! Applying the holy correction of forgiveness will vaporize all that appears to change, in the chaotic world you now perceive. It will release of misery and destruction, scarcity and senseless attacks while restoring you to awareness of everpresent Truth and unconditional Love. Then the natural radiance, within your mind, will shine effortlessly forth, having dispelled all sources of ignorance.

AWAKENING THE SLEEPING GIANT

(Sharon) How can I more judiciously awaken and empower the gencept of Truth into my life?

(Jesus) The gencept of Truth is representative of a knowledge and power that never sleeps. One that remains widely awake within the subaqueous expanses of your unconscious mind. Its wisdom is deeply assimilated into the very fabric of your being. However, you have lost access to its endless streams of vitalizing influence because your conscious mind has become blind. You can no longer see a thing in its true radiance and natural splendor because of all that trashy worldly knowledge that stands in your way. All that, which you have intellectually formulated and symbolized.

The gencept of Truth's towering vastness, degree of abstraction and world-shattering scope render it unseen. Since it underpins an entire field of potentialities, its true face can never be depicted in the world of specifics. For it is not any manifest appearance but extends far beyond their reach. Each particular world of form you perceive is merely a distortion arising from your endowment of the gencept of error. This automatically relegates you to a very opaque and narrow-banded state of conscious evolution.

Thus the giant remains in slumber. You must raise its wisdom to conscious awareness through an evolution in your psyche. You must dive deep within, and raise your awareness to such a heightened intensity and depth, that the latent can be revealed. The world of specifics can be employed very advantageously as a valuable tool to apprehend that which is beyond them. Once you can diagnose the same content abiding in many different forms, the gencept of Truth will begin to emerge into view.

Content is its gift to you and this needs to be unmasked. You must become capable of reaching far more abstract and generalized understandings. Only then, will the higher operating manifold behind the curtains of form, be brought into the light. When your mind has become so expert and advanced in its image projection capabilities, it will unveil the hidden dimensions. Once you evolve past the abacus of concepts, the calculus of the supra-conceptual will be clearly fathomed and appreciated for all its elegance. The intention is to steer deeper in the direction of essence. This higher dimensional capability is just reflective of your becoming more attuned to Knowledge. Associative visualization techniques are a mighty and influential tool to expose all errors and contradictions. Their application portends vastly accelerated learning potential for you.

Ignorance is not bliss! What you deny can be very damaging to both yourself and others. Denial makes you into a slave of that which is repressed. It establishes a destructive chain of reactionary mentation which then rules over your mind. One that automatically directs all your decisions and actions while insidiously poisoning the well of your mind with its wicked persuasions. Your ignorance can become so twisted and convoluted in its conceit that it morphs into a tyrannical dictator who then determines all that you will accept or judge against.

What you judge against then disappears out of view. The eyes of your denial, amplify all your preferences producing an imaginary world, that has nothing to do with truth. The gencept of Truth is available but is covered over by all your denials, arbitrary wishes, and false knowledge. You can activate it into view, by raising all that is denied and exposing all false beliefs to the light of your conscious awareness. This is the light that heals by shining the unreal away.

THE 3-D WORLD AS A QUANTUM POTENTIALITY

(Sharon) What is the relationship between the 3-D world of our perceptions and the Gencept?

(Jesus) The 3-D world, you perceive it just the actualization of one quantum potentiality. It represents just one appearance your state of consciousness has collapsed into seeming existence. Each such materialization only has a pseudo-reality, being a dream of the mind. Nevertheless, all quantum potentialities are of the same order of validity. Some manifest into worlds and others do not. Your mind could just as easily have collapsed into visible existence an alternate potentiality. It is, therefore, wise to draw no distinction between actualities and potentialities. Both are essentially mirages and mere slices of a hyper-dimensional world, which you cannot yet grasp. Each pertains to a dream landscape and inherently reflects all your thought distortions, self-deceptions, and desires.

Gencepts encompass an infinite set of such potentialities, all packaged neatly into arrays of 3-D worlds. The particular slice you see is due to waveform collapse of one of an infinite series of quantum possibilities. Your current evolutionary state of consciousness can only competently illuminate one 3-D landscape, at a time.

Your mind, being dualistically framed, does not possess the fluidity yet to dissolve all its illusory partitions. You cannot fathom therefore the raw power of the gencept, because if you could, you would peer beyond them and witness higher dimensional worlds. So you experience, a seemingly infinite set of consciousness/perception dyads, all laden with error. Each representing a partialized picture of that which is immanent and transcendent to all world potentialities. Your ideational streams cannot differentiate between the manifest and unmanifest. All consciousness must distort to some extent, so forming icebergs in the sea of formlessness. What is perceived is not the truth. It just represents your many preferences and judgments.

PERFECT UNDERSTANDING

(Sharon) What is the fastest and best way to reach Perfect Understanding?

(Jesus) Perfect understanding is attained through the correction of error. You must fully realize that the original error, has now spread its contagion pervasively through the entire framework of your thought. It has embedded you deeply in the dream of ignorance. One in which, you continue to uphold false dualistic notions. However, once the myth of dualism is exposed, your healing can soon cascade to have a monumental impact. Then your mind will no longer picture a fragmented world because it will be illuminated through its own perfect thought. So you will witness the non-transient essence and infinite intelligence that binds all. This then ends all nonsensical questions of the ego forever and brings its reign to an end.

Enlightened Mind is not fooled by all inferior notions and concepts indigenous to 3-D thinking. It knows that unity can never be comprehended by those who entertain false divisions. That the senses are the greatest liars because they speak so loudly of a world that is not there. It is cogently aware that all boundaries and differentiations are fictional and the world of appearances just mirrors one's mindset. Nor is it deceived by false notions concerning bodies, space and seemingly "separated" minds. Likewise, it knows that all sickness and suffering are mirages arising from erroneous thought.

It makes no distinctions between the inner and outer since it knows that Being has no spatial direction. It compellingly understands that the illusory is powerless forever to subtract, even a jot, from the Sovereignty of Truth.

UNMASKING THE GENCEPT OF ERROR

(Sharon) Can you furnish me with a full etiological breakdown on both the cause and progression path of the Gencept of Error?

(Jesus) The gencept of error began with the tiny-mad-idea (TMI). Before that unholy instant, there was no stain of impure thought in the Mind of God's Son. The refulgent perfection of Whole-Mind alone was known. The guilt associated with this idea gave birth to the ego and brought into play the dissociative experience of split-mind. Both of which grew proportionately, as the impurity spread to affect all crannies of our mind and thought. Those parts, our minds rejected became projected as images which then formed into the landscape of our perception. Interpreting our existence as separate, gave birth to our conscious modes of experiencing.

Our defiled state of mind immediately lost all awareness of Truth and had to experience its existence serially and in a fragmented fashion. In short, we readily felt ourselves immersed in the world of spacetime, bodies and so much junk. Severely blinded by our warped misunderstandings, we found it extremely strenuous to discern the veracious elements in the perceptual frames that were continuously being streamed our way. Consequently, that one error unleashed a veritable rat's nest of all that was foul and fair, before our eyes. Soon the world became carved out of our arbitrary judgments and driven by our preferences and wild desires. Our projecting mindset, in its futile attempt to make sense of it all, decided to disown its projections. Then desperate to claim innocence made these the sources of all guilt.

This induced certain strange and toxic beliefs into the mind, all of which promptly took up residence in the lower chambers. They established an insurmountable fortress of defensive hyper-structures around themselves to guarantee their alien tenancy would never be exposed or opposed. They swore to protect the vested interests of their lord and master, the ego.

The mind became covered over by a dark impenetrable cloud. Out of this cloud emerged the body. The ego was delighted because this newfangled novelty served to ensure all its desired illusions for separation would remain intact. Its greatest fantasy had been fulfilled. Its mythical existence would now go unquestioned because your thought was too deeply sunk in the swamp of the world. All the same, it decided the best way to keep you from interrogating it was to have some exotic carnivals of flesh and sidewalk freak shows every now and then. So it sent you off into the world of perception with the noble goals of extracting as much pleasure, as you could and to exhibit your body's specialness to all. However with the body came notions of impermanence and the first appearances of sickness, suffering, and loss. All of which led onwards to the illusion of death. Before that, death was inconceivable.

No idea stands alone! Each one we cherish threads its way thoroughly through our conceptual, perceptual and sensory existence. Very much shaping the world, we perceive while instantiating false images over the immaculate and faceless. The gencept of error, once invested in, gained in its power to deceive us. So we came to believe in the power of nothingness and found ourselves lost and trapped in the world's dim scope.

(Sharon) It all seems so intricate and conceptually elegant that I am going to draw a diagram that depicts the full chain of cause-and-effect proceeding from the TMI to the bodily illusion and death.

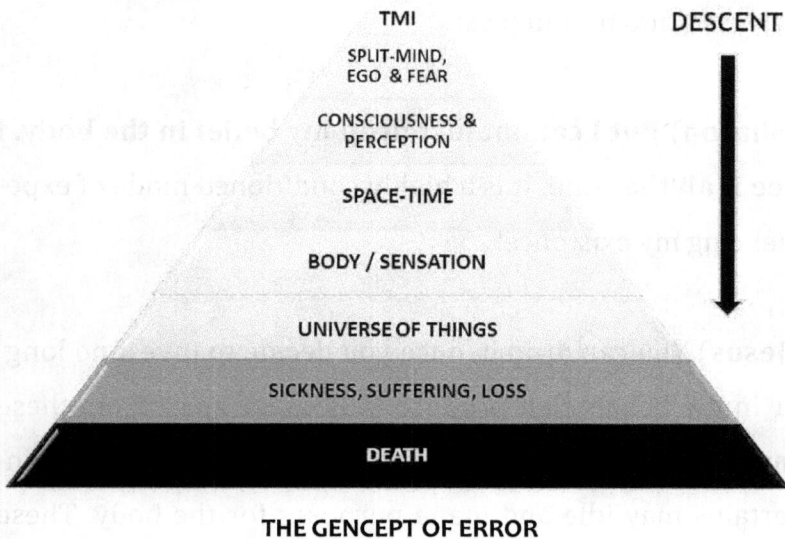

TMI   DESCENT

SPLIT-MIND,
EGO & FEAR

CONSCIOUSNESS &
PERCEPTION

SPACE-TIME

BODY / SENSATION

UNIVERSE OF THINGS

SICKNESS, SUFFERING, LOSS

DEATH

THE GENCEPT OF ERROR

(Jesus) Excellent Work! Your gencept diagram is very comprehensive since it accounts for some of its physical manifestations, but also extends to the meta-real and finally to the mentally abstract. Like, any poorly designed skyscraper, this gencept can topple and fall, once it is found to be built on nothing but a sandcastle of illusions. It does not matter at which layer you decide to place your stick of dynamite.

For example, once you drop all belief in the body, your spacetime experience will also come to an end. Because your spacetime experiencing is contingent on having a body, to experience it with. Without spacetime, all conscious experience will likewise end. Nor can the ego long survive and thrive without your bodily belief, and so it is released into nothingness.

(Sharon) But I cannot just drop my belief in the body. I see it all the time. It is a highly conditioned mode of experiencing my existence!

(Jesus) You can drop it, once you decide to invest no longer in the beliefs that produce it. Because apart from these investments, it has never been. For example, your ego entertains may idle and inane purposes for the body. These

include physical temptations such as pleasure, and adorn-
ment, and psychological temptations such as its beliefs in
specialness, sin, and guilt. So it avails of the body both to
survive in your mind and to keep all illusions of separation
reinforced. It knows, that so long as you worship the body,
and give in to its temptations you are freely entering its
prison-house of fear. Then alone, it feels safe because it
knows you will treasure all that nonsense, it incessantly
vociferates. Once you conceive of fear, as a reality, all concepts of divine Love must go out the window. Yes, unconditional Love will seem like some cruel joke, because who
can believe in a world of terror and vengeance and still regard Love as Real?

No, your mind will accord reality to one alone, once you
have entered the gates to the ego's self-styled paradise.
Then the one, you do not choose becomes merely a façade.
An idle word to be thrown about at parties to impress your
friends. Maybe they will buy into your ruse and think you
are human after all, and not a monster. The outcome of all
this is God gets to be seen a deceptive imposter. A cold,
cruelhearted monster who has mercilessly thrown you on
the mud-pile of the world. A place of festering misery, with
no hope ever of escape. However, as I said in the past:-

"The fear of God is fear of life, and not of death.

Yet He remains the only place of safety. In Him

is no attack, and no illusion in any form stalks

Heaven."

[ACIM, T-23,IV.1:2-4]

Your misplaced beliefs do not make for truth. You can easily expose all such ego myths through either reason or by dropping all bodily investments. The first step is recognizing how empty and superficial all bodily temptations are. They must always disappoint. For example, the silent appeals of sin and guilt keep you isolated, sick and fearful of attack. As a result, you find it very challenging to communicate honestly and transparently with those around you. Your attraction to physical pleasure always induces an equal amount of pain and your desire for specialness forces you to chop heads. Nevertheless, your superiority never lasts, because it is not real.

Relinquishing all these foolish investments will lead to those pivotal mystical experiences, in which you will witness the body disappear. So it will dissipate into the mists of your vaporous consciousness when you desire it no longer. It cannot long substantiate its existence without your continued investment in it.

Reason tells you that the body is powerless to perceive because it, itself, is a perception. The body, therefore, cannot be its own cause. So what is this mysterious power that is perceiving it? Isn't it your conscious mind? A mind laden with so many senseless wishes, including the desires for attack! One so profoundly split, that it now perceives, as real, an illusionary effect spawned from its own thinking? So the body and the entire world of objects are just projections of conditioned beliefs, deeply woven into the fabric of your thought. Collectively these can be labeled as ignorance, and they lead to your perpetual state of confusion.

Unbiased reason works because it cuts through all illusions and belief distortions. It empowers you to uproot the underlying gencept of error, in all its many faces and guises. You will stand mystified that you had never laid bare the deeper ideational connections before. You had always thought of beliefs, as lone wolves, out on the ice pack, existing independently of all others. Now you see this nexus of insidious ideas operates more like a pack of wolves. So each idea in a gencept leaves a genetic imprint, which can be used to trace its full lineage.

(Sharon) But why does the Gencept of Error survive so pervasively in our minds?

(Jesus) All ideas in a gencept support all their siblings. To nourish one, is to resuscitate and invigorate the entire organism of deception. Your attraction to any of its elements strengthens your conviction in the whole. Taken together, they form an impenetrable network of belief, just as a sheaf of stalks or reeds can be woven into a very enduring fabric of strength and resilience. The very widespread and polymorphic nature of the gencept makes it extremely potent indeed because it furnishes it with the capacity to stitch and cross-associates all its ideas in an unbroken chain.

For example, wherever fear is present judgment is quickly turned into a retaliatory weapon of self-protection. This increases the initial fear and leads onwards to beliefs in victimization. Then follows a need to instantiate copious defenses. Your belief in victimization places you in a state of displacement, from correct understanding, because victimhood declares all power is on the outside, rather than within. So it seems to relegate the projecting mind into a diminutive figure of its own dream.

This, in turn, perpetuates your state of dreaming and strong ego identification. Feeling vulnerable as a dream figure, you begin to believe sickness and suffering have external causes. You completely forget they are merely miscreations of mind. Your solution for your sad predicament is to project your mind-power to various magical remedies and healing technologies. Examined and probed closer, you discern that fear does not arise in a vacuum. It correlates closely to your other beliefs, including those of separation and of existing in a body. All the same, you alone invented this world of separation through your attempts at guilt alleviation. So you are the only architect of all fear. Once you correctly identify and cross-associate some of the ideas sharing the same gencept, you quickly begin to detect them all.

(Sharon) I will see, if I can insert some more related ideas into my original diagram for the gencept of error!

TMI

GUILT

DESCENT

SPLIT-MIND,
EGO & FEAR

CONSCIOUSNESS &
PERCEPTION

SPACE-TIME

BODY, SENSATION, MISCREATION

EVOLVING CONTRASTS,
DIFFERENTIATIONS

UNIVERSE OF THINGS, IDOLS, DESIRES

PERPETUAL DREAMING and EGO IDENTIFICATION

JUDGMENT, CONDEMNATION, ATTACK, DEFENSE, SIN

SICKNESS, SUFFERING, SACRIFICE, LOSS, MAGICAL BELIEFS

DEATH

THE GENCEPT OF ERROR (EXPANDED)

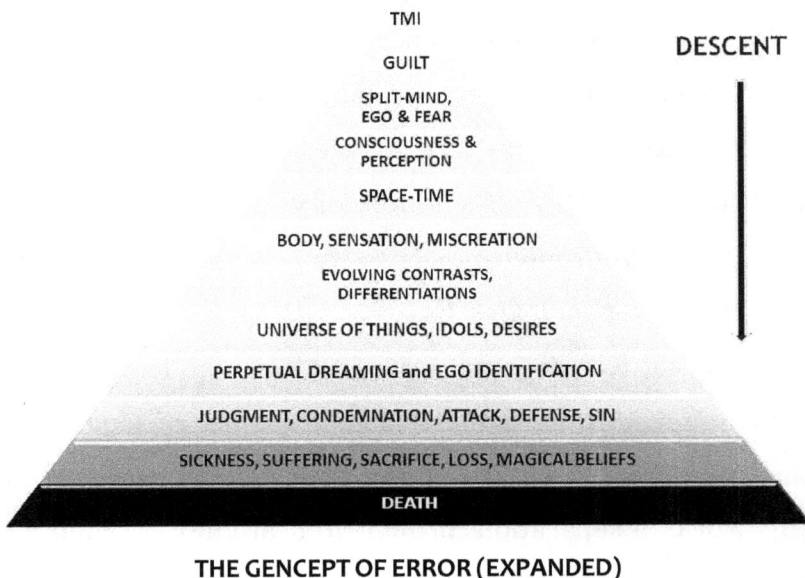

(Jesus) Once you cease to believe in any of the ideas, the entire framework begins to fall. Once the empty and false content is exposed anywhere, it becomes quickly divested of all its ideational energy and force. For example, when you know guilt has no real basis, you will cease to project it. As a consequence, your beliefs in judgment and sin will soon lose all attraction. Without these to distort, the underlying unity of existence becomes apparent, and so all boundaries, contrasts, and differentiations melt away. Now you know these were ego hells of delusion arising from your use of this retaliatory weapon both to protect yourself and to prove your specialness.

For the first time, you begin to feel your true invulnerability of mind. So you lose all interest in maintaining your bodily fence, as well as with all magical potions. As these become purposeless, fear finds no means by which to refuel itself. It now becomes abundantly evident that you are the deathless mind that projects the dream and Love, long denied, is now made welcome again!

By mapping out the gencept, you begin to trace connections that weren't overtly obvious before. For example, the link between fear and judgment is easily recognizable but the common thread shared between fear, and your dreaming state is not readily apparent. It would be difficult also, to grasp the link between consciousness and suffering without the help of a gencept diagram. With all gencepts, the essential bedrock remains the same, even when the individual faces can seem so diverse and Medusa like. The gencept chart empowers one to behold the underlying reality that joins many seemingly divergent ideas together. One grasps, how a single seemingly innocuous belief can trigger and reinforce a whole set of connecting beliefs and can spread far and wide.

The gencept of error is the gencept of darkness and nothingness. It has no real power. All its apparent power derives from the certitude your mind lends to it, through accrediting faith to its vast network of interconnected beliefs. Drop your faith in any of its ideas and it can be severely weakened. Do it with conviction, and all its effects instantly disappear. In the end, it will be either accepted whole or rejected whole. Retain belief in any of associated ideas and you choose continued bondage to the ego over your freedom.

THE GENCEPT OF TRUTH

(Sharon) How does the Gencept of Truth Compare?

(Jesus) The gencept of Truth is that of light, healing, inspiration, miracles and experiences of heavenly unity. It restores awareness of innocence and transports one into the arms of unconditional love and joy. Through it, all conflicts disappear and one is reinstated to the perfect understanding of Whole-Mind. All ideas in this gencept stand in stark contrast to those portrayed by the gencept of error. For example, the ego belief in death is superseded with knowledge of everlasting life, sickness and suffering are overtaken by glowing health and the world of objects dislodged by recognition of formlessness. Just as the ego thrived in the body and the world of sensation, one now indulges fulltime in Spiritual Bliss.

The spacetime existence starts to dematerialize, and the Real world of light and Revelatory experiences comes increasingly into view. The world of time becomes powerless now to hold back the reality of Truth, just as the fading night cannot long withstand the bright rays of the morning Sun. For every dark and nebulous concept present in the gencept of error, there is a corresponding glorious and effulgent counter-thought in the gencept of Truth that portends your complete release.

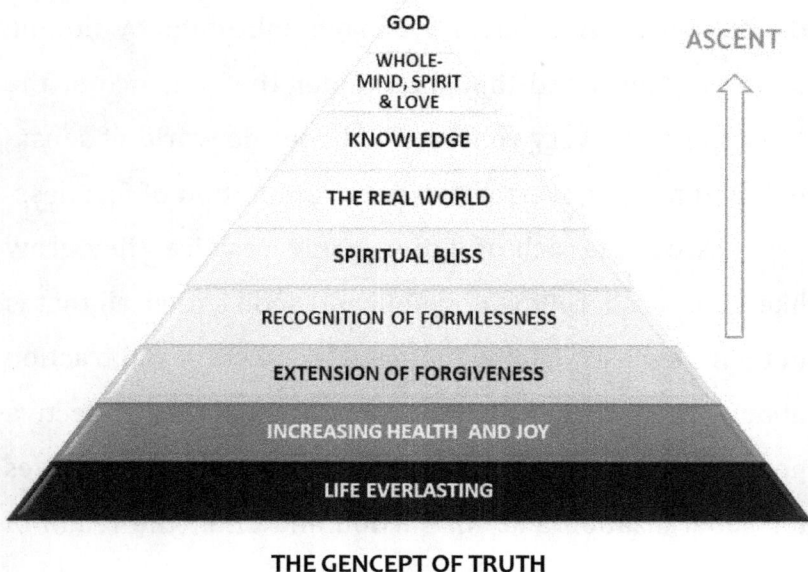

GOD

WHOLE-
MIND, SPIRIT
& LOVE

ASCENT

KNOWLEDGE

THE REAL WORLD

SPIRITUAL BLISS

RECOGNITION OF FORMLESSNESS

EXTENSION OF FORGIVENESS

INCREASING HEALTH AND JOY

LIFE EVERLASTING

THE GENCEPT OF TRUTH

Its Knowledge reminds us that eternal life is not something we have to earn, but part of our divine inheritance. Once we learn to forgive and bless, we become restored to lasting happiness and health. As our minds are cleansed of all ego distortions, our spiritual understanding starts to run crystal clear. Our newfound clarity and transparency then empower a healing light to burst forth. Losing all thoughts of separation, we are granted a supreme vision of the supra-conceptual and unified existence. This light then pours outward into our perceptions, providing a welcome foretaste of our heavenly paradise. We enter the happy dream, which is the precursor to our awakening.

This gencept offers us a progression path back to God and the bliss of the Absolute. It heals our split-mind by ridding us of all guilt-based thoughts. Under the guidance of the Holy Spirit, the very concrete and specific world of sensation and form is overthrown with recognition of formlessness. As we put each of its ideas into practice, they grow like a snowball, rolling downhill and soon gather all that is in their likeness. Gaining increased conviction and traction in our thoughts, they likewise strengthen in their collective power. So our minds evolve to ever-increased capacities for generalization and abstraction and enter the realm of the supra-conceptual.

Increasingly divested of error, we become reintegrated and healed, until finally the pure awareness of Whole-Mind alone is known. Meanwhile, love's impartiality unbinds us further from the world of specifics and is now given universal application. So it is that the dream of spacetime and form comes to an end and Truth alone remains. All because we made the simple and clearcut decision for Atonement.

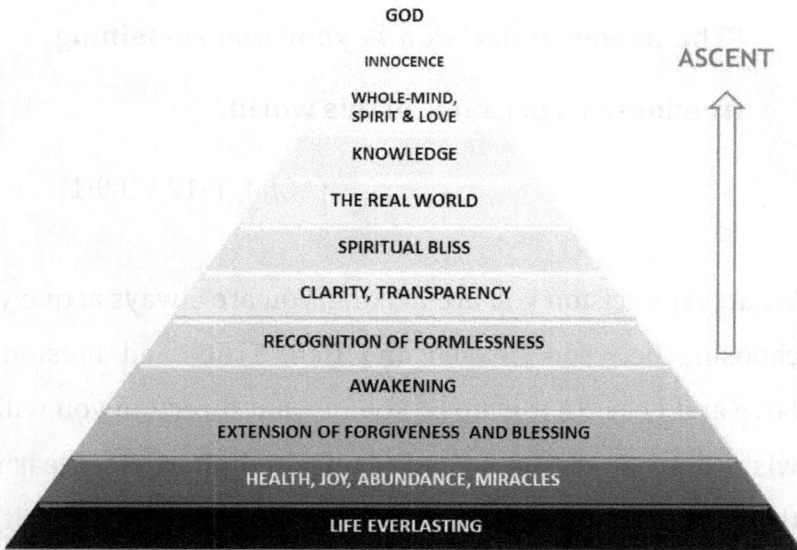

GOD

INNOCENCE   ASCENT

WHOLE-MIND, SPIRIT & LOVE

KNOWLEDGE

THE REAL WORLD

SPIRITUAL BLISS

CLARITY, TRANSPARENCY

RECOGNITION OF FORMLESSNESS

AWAKENING

EXTENSION OF FORGIVENESS AND BLESSING

HEALTH, JOY, ABUNDANCE, MIRACLES

LIFE EVERLASTING

THE GENCEPT OF TRUTH (EXPANDED)

THE ONLY SANE DECISION

(Sharon) How important is the wise execution of our Power of Decision in all this?

(Jesus) All your decisions are crucial. As I said in the Course:-

"The power of decision is your one remaining freedom as a prisoner of this world."

[ACIM, T-12.VII.9:1]

Whatever decision you are making, you are always actively choosing between Heaven and Hell, Truth and Illusion, Love and Fear. So it is up to you in what direction you will wish to proceed. You can so readily and effortlessly learn the power of light over darkness, innocence over guilt, abundance over scarcity, and Spirit over the ego's tyranny. It all comes down to what you want! There is no essential difference between what you believe and what you want to believe. This is because the ego will always rationalize its beliefs based on its desires alone. Are you happy with the world you see or are you ready for something completely different, vibrant and new? Some glorious mind-blowing recognition, from which you will never turn back?

The ego has set many deadly snares to attract your mind. All poisonous bait strategically placed, to hook you. Then it will lock you securely inside its prison-house and throw away the keys. The attractions of guilt, sin, and judgment, name but a few of it allurements. Then there are the countless temptations of the body, the ego's endless enumeration of idols and its dreams of specialness. But these all inevitably lead to feelings of vulnerability, weakness, and fear, forcing you cave to its beliefs in sickness and the need for magical remedies. You become so paranoid, as not to venture out of doors, preferring to hide instead behind a mind-numbing array of its futile defenses.

Alternatively, you could have masterfully chosen sanity and health and full recognition of the power of your thought and decision. An unswerving and dedicated practice of defenselessness would have taught you your freedom and provided increased awareness of your invulnerability.

Do not look to the world of perception for answers! Because it is riddled all over with faithful witnesses to sickness, fear, loss, and death. All the same, this unfortunate tragicomedy with all its excessive, tasteless and sententious dramatizations can never succeed in making any of its effects real. It merely represents what you have taught yourself in the past and reflects the natural outcome of your choosing with the ego.

Though chaos, meaninglessness, and confusion rain down upon you and a million different forms rise to tempt and tantalize, remember the only gap ever-existing is between Truth and your awareness of it. All such effects are like the chiaroscuro of low flying cloud and can but temporarily rise to block out the Sun of Truth. What never happened, cannot be difficult to release!

The question remains, will you continue to believe in time or extend a little faith, for once, to the Eternal? For only one can be the final Truth! Either eternity is fact and time a vast illusion or time is real and death an inescapable certainty. Either you remain changeless, perfect and immortal forever or death is the final arbitrator over all life. Either all things die, or else they live and cannot die. There can never be any compromise between these two positions!

Meanwhile, your mind, caught in its twisted web of deceptions continuously flips and flops and ends up making no progress at all. Endlessly vacillating, it remains at ransom to the world of dreams. Your failure to blaze a pathway towards Truth is the decision to go nowhere. Only a darkened mind, wandering idly along the hallways of ignorance can still believe this is a wise choice. Having temporarily lost all capacity to discriminate and reason it still thinks there are equally valid options, on either side.

The only other question then, is when will you become hungry and despairing enough, to accept no longer, the ego's vain imaginings in place of your Reality? Tire of eating that empty space, which is the carcass of perception? Become ready to make the only sane choice and plant your first footsteps on the bridge of Atonement? The one that leads most decidedly away from the gencept of error and into the Real World. Choose Atonement, and you will soon find yourself at Home, embraced in the arms of unconditional Love and Peace. Your mind radiant, joyful and awake, having overcome its sickness.

Other Books by Sharon Moriarty

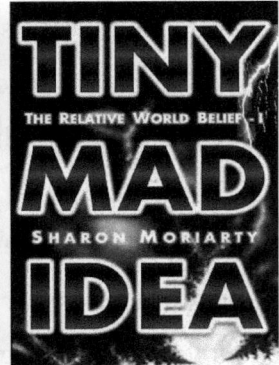

E-Books and Paperbacks Available now on Amazon and CreateSpace.

http://www.Amazon.com

ABOUT THE AUTHORS

Sharon Moriarty is a Yogi, Mystic, and Adventurer. In her past lives, she professionally engaged in Hardware Engineering, Management, Lecturing, Software Development, and Sales. She enjoys sharing her insights and wisdom on the Course material and communicating its ideas in a very lucid and in-depth manner. She places particular emphasis on the practical application of the Course Principles and hopes you enjoy your Spiritual journey.

Jesus Christ is a Healer and Savior and has been deputized by God to be in charge of the Atonement. He is the silent channeling Authority behind **"A Course In Miracles"** and has also been commended for his miracle working abilities, capacities to alleviate all suffering and pain and for his resurrection. Doing so, he compellingly proved the power of life over all darkness, death, and transience.

He is also very practical by nature, having worked part-time as a carpenter, fisherman and wine producer. This practical dimension is evident in the 365 Spiritually Transformative Course Lessons; he has provided for our Salvation. His present words of advice to all those Dreambound are :

"Teach not that I died in vain. Teach rather that I did not die by demonstrating that I live in you."